INSIDER TIPS, TRICKS, AND STRATEGIES
FOR SELLING MORE BOOKS

THE
AMAZON
AUTHOR
FORMULA

PENNY C.
SANSEVIERI

MORE BOOKS BY PENNY C. SANSEVIERI

NONFICTION

5 Minute Book Marketing for Authors (Amazon Digital 2018, 2019)

52 Ways to Sell More Books (Amazon Digital 2014, 2019)

How to Sell Books by the Truckload on Amazon.com (Amazon Digital 2013, 2018, 2019, 2020, 2021, 2022)

50 Ways to Sell a Sleigh-Load of Books: Proven Marketing Strategies to Sell More Books for the Holidays (Amazon Digital 2018)

How to Revise and Re-Release Your Book: Simple and Smart Strategies to Sell More Books (Amazon Digital 2018)

Red Hot Internet Publicity - 4th Edition (Amazon Digital 2016)

How to Get a Truckload of Reviews on Amazon.com (Amazon Digital 2013)

Red Hot Internet Publicity (Createspace 2013)

Powerful Pinterest (Amazon Digital 2012)

Get Published Today (Wheatmark, 2012)

52 Ways to Sell More Books (Wheatmark, 2012)

Red Hot Internet Publicity (Cosimo 2010)

Red Hot Internet Publicity (Morgan James Publishing 2007)

From Book to Bestseller (Morgan James Publishing, 2007)

Get Published Today (Morgan James Publishing, 2007)

From Book to Bestseller (PublishingGold.com, Inc., 2005)

No More Rejections: Get Published Today! (Infinity Publishing, 2002, 2003)

Get Published! An Author's Guide to the Online Publishing Revolution (1st Books, 2001)

FICTION

Candlewood Lake (iUniverse, 2005)
The Cliffhanger (iUniverse, 2000)

We'd love to hear your feedback.
Here's how to contact us:

AUTHOR MARKETING EXPERTS

Author Marketing Experts, Inc.
10601-G Tierrasanta Blvd., Suite 458
San Diego, CA 92124
www.amarketingexpert.com

CONTENTS

PART ONE
YOUR AMAZON SEARCH RANKING

PART TWO
YOUR AMAZON BOOK PAGE

PART THREE
SUCCESSFUL BOOK LAUNCHES ON AMAZON

PART FOUR
ROCKETING YOUR BOOK TO SUCCESS WITH AMAZON ADVERTISING

PART FIVE

AMAZON ADS—THE BASICS

HOW TO USE THIS BOOK

As of this writing there are approximately eight million books on the Amazon site, with more being added every day. According to best estimates, 8,216 books are published each day in the United States, yet only 1% of those authors bother to spend any time optimizing their Amazon page.

What does this mean for you? It means that if you implement just one strategy from this book, you're way ahead of most of the authors out there vying for reader attention.

The most efficient way to use this book is to read it from start to finish. But if you're in a rush to acquire some particular knowledge (like the newly updated Amazon Ads section), then feel free to jump ahead. If you're new to the ideas of keywords, keyword strings, and enhanced Amazon categories, spend some time in the early chapters getting familiar with terminology and the way the Amazon algorithm works.

If you're already an Amazon expert and are just here to brush up on your knowledge, then feel free to scan the chapter headings, which are divided in microfashion to allow for easy skimming.

I hope you enjoy this book, and I'd love your thoughts on it, either in a review on Amazon or in a direct email to me: penny@amarketingexpert.com

Wishing you huge Amazon success!

NEW NAME. SAME FABULOUS CONTENT.

I can't believe it's been 10 years since the first edition of my Amazon marketing book was published. For 10 years I've published under the "truckload" umbrella. Multiple books, webinars, and digital content were created under the truckload brand. But now I think it's time to change it up, to really shake things up (as Amazon often does to authors with its ever-changing algorithm). So welcome to *The Amazon Author Formula*. A new edition, a new look, but still digging deep into demystifying all things Amazon.

If you've been with me on this journey for the last 10 years, thank you. I'm sure you know how things have changed. From Amazon's humble beginnings in a garage to where it is now—I don't know if anyone could have imagined it.

If this is your first time reading one of my books, thank you! I hope you'll find this not only helpful, but accessible and easy to understand as well as implement.

So if you're ready, let's dig in.

PART ONE
YOUR AMAZON SEARCH RANKING

AMAZON'S SEARCH STRUCTURE EXPLAINED

To begin a book about ranking on Amazon, we first have to understand how the Amazon search function works. This is also a good place to explain its algorithm. All of this will help you as you begin to work through the chapters in this book.

But understanding how Amazon's search function works is the foundation of everything we're about to learn.

It's not an overstatement to say that Amazon has changed everything about book publishing and promotion. It seems like every time Amazon introduces something, the competition jumps on the bandwagon and creates similar products or experiences on their sites.

This is a problem because the Amazon ecosystem is a tremendous game changer. Much like Google, it can not only help you find exactly the book you've been looking for; it can also show you things you never knew you needed.

That's the power of the algorithm, and it's also the power of the ads.

I've talked about how alike Amazon and Google are, which makes sense when you consider that Jeff Bezos was an early investor in Google and had an inside track to learn how Google worked as it developed into the behemoth it is today. Actually, the algorithms of Google and Amazon are quite similar.

But dissecting and understanding Amazon is like dismantling a house brick by brick. No one person can do that, but we can uncover various algorithms that can help you achieve more visibility for your book.

When it comes to Amazon, there are no quick fixes. There's no single solution; instead, all of the features work in tandem. And there are several strategies that help create optimal visibility for your book.

While many experts talk about keyword strings, categories, and pricing, few experts mention this important fact:

Amazon is more of a search engine than it is a store. In fact, Amazon is the "Google" of online buying.

And with this model in mind, I need to stress that there is no instant anything when it comes to ranking on Amazon. There's an abundance of shortcut software out there, and keyword apps, but time and time again, I've been reminded that there's nothing like good old-fashioned hard work to make your Amazon page soar. People are always searching for shortcuts, but they rarely work.

Understanding Amazon and knowing how to use it to your advantage are vital to keeping those sales up. Amazon is *the* place for book marketing today. All the way back in June of 2014, *SEOMoz*, a popular search engine optimization blog, talked about Amazon and its ranking system. It said, "If you're an author, you don't care about ranking on Google. You want to rank on Amazon."

THINKING IN SEARCH ENGINE TERMS

As you'll learn, the work you do on Amazon to promote your book is similar to what I would recommend if you were trying to get traction on Google for your website. This is the mindset you must embrace. Unfortunately, I haven't found discussions of this mindset in many of the books I've read on this topic.

Therein lies another problem.

When the first edition of this book came out, there were dozens of book on the market about how to sell on Amazon books. Now the number has dwindled to just a few.

Why? I think a lot of it has to do with the fact that Amazon is tough to monitor. The algorithm changes a lot, and it's essential to keep an eye on it if you want your book to be successful.

So, back to our search engine mindset. Let's compare the website requirements for ranking on Google vs. the Amazon requirements for your book.

To get Google ranking for your website, you need a few things:

1. Metadata: Keyword strings that your market is searching for.
2. An attractive website: The days of Google ranking bad-looking sites are over. Today you need an attractive website. I don't mean pretty, just no sloppy train wrecks cobbled together without a purpose or user-friendly navigation.
3. Consistent blog posts: Google likes this because it tells Google the site is being updated frequently, which helps your search results.

Now, if we turn to Amazon, and translate this to book/product speak, we see that similar rules apply:

1. Metadata: Keywords, keywords, keywords—Amazon loves keywords (i.e., keyword strings), and applying that knowledge skillfully will help you achieve better ranking.
2. A strong book cover: While Amazon may not ding you for a bad-looking cover, your potential readers most certainly will.

3. Reviews: Consistently getting new reviews is likened to regularly blogging on your website. It shows there's consistent activity. Reviews also help with the visibility of your page and your ranking on Amazon, even if your book is several years old.
4. Amazon Ads: We'll dig into this more in Part Five of this book.
5. Book page: Much like your website, your Amazon book page should be peppered with keywords.

Since you're just beginning to understand the ins and outs of optimization, this is the foundation that will guide you to creating an outstanding Amazon book page, with Amazon ads that complement everything you're doing and push the consumer to buy.

But before we dig into more keywords, categories, and optimization, let's first look at Amazon's relevancy score.

AMAZON'S RELEVANCY SCORE AND WHY EVERYTHING MATTERS

When I teach authors about websites and how to optimize them for maximum visibility on Google, I remind people that absolutely everything matters to Google. To get a great search rank, leave no stone unturned. Every page, every keyword, every image counts for or against you in terms of ranking.

The same is true with Amazon.

"Relevancy score" is my term; it's not something Amazon has shared with me, but it makes sense because that's how Google ranks.

Let me explain.

Google's number one goal is to get its consumers to the right website. If your website is coming up under Vegan Cooking, but your site doesn't serve that market well – or consumers are clicking on your site but not spending much time on it, that negatively impacts your relevancy score, and Google will keep dropping your site down the search rank until it's on page five of Google.

I often say if you want to hide a dead body, bury it on page five of Google because no one goes there anyway.

So how does Amazon's relevancy score work?

Let's say you're running some Facebook ads and you're getting lots of clicks, but no sales. This tells Amazon your book isn't relevant to the search, and that will impact your search rank on Amazon.

Really?

Yes, really.

Amazon's goal is to serve up things its consumers want to buy; the site isn't there for window shoppers, and the website is quite intelligent. If someone lands on your book page and immediately clicks off without engaging with your page at all (expanding your book description to reach more, scrolling down to read the reviews), that tells Amazon your book isn't right for the market; consequently, it becomes harder to rank. So if you're thinking about your own Facebook ads (or even your Amazon ads) that are getting lots of clicks but no buys, you may want to consider how it's impacting your relevancy score and your overall visibility on Amazon.

I'll go into this more when we start digging into your Amazon book page because when authors tell me their ads aren't working, I can almost guarantee you it's because of their Amazon book page.

So, how far back does Amazon go when considering your overall relevancy score?

Remember that first book you published that didn't do well? The cover wasn't great—you knew it could have or should have been better—but it was your first book, so you took it in stride. You learned from your mistakes and you moved on.

The thing is, Amazon never moves on. Somewhere, lurking in the back end of Amazon is a black mark beside your name, and that mark means, *This author once published a book no one seemed to like = low relevancy.*

Amazon cares about relevancy. It's how the entire site—with all of its millions of products—manages to find exactly the thing you're looking for when you need it. Plug in a few keywords and, *boom*, the exact widget, lotion, or book you were looking for appears. This is why relevancy is so important and why making sure everything connected to your Amazon account (even the older books you've published) is in tiptop shape. This point can't be overemphasized.

The other element of this as it relates to Amazon ads is that the less conversion you have on your Amazon book page (i.e., the lower your relevancy score), the more your ads will cost you. And if your ads never seem to do well across the board, Amazon will ding your relevancy score as well. If you have an ad set that's not doing well, kill it. We'll go more in depth on this later in the ads section.

Is there any hope for that older book that didn't do well? Fortunately, there are some options. Often, it means revisiting an older title, maybe republishing it, revamping the cover, or in extreme cases, taking it down entirely. But that's pretty much a last resort.

A few years ago I noticed that our website (www. amarketingexpert.com) wasn't ranking as well as it should for the term "book marketing." Considering that that's the work we do, it's a pretty important term to rank for. Upon investigation, I discovered that a page on our website was broken. By "broken," I mean it had no keywords, no title tags; it was basically a mess. I fixed it and within about three months, our website was back and ranking again.

You can use the same method for an older book: fix what needs fixing and show Amazon that you mean business. The algorithm keeps a close eye on fixes, updates, and any polishing you do to your book or book page and quickly notes, This author means business.

If you're ready for more ideas, head on over to Part Two of this book where we'll really dig into your Amazon book page.

For now, just remember that each piece of the Amazon puzzle impacts the other pieces, and everything you do impacts everything else. It all matters. The good news? It's easier than ever to get back on track, and small changes and enhancements can help build your status in the Amazon ecosystem and grow your presence for both your author page and your book pages.

UNDERSTANDING KEYWORDS AND WHY THEY MATTER

When I teach this class in person, this is often when I see authors tune out. The entire topic of keywords and finding the right keywords is confusing to most people, and we know that a confused mind zones out. So, if you feel like you've read a lot on this topic but can't seem to absorb it, you're not alone.

To explain this topic in a way that isn't geek speak and doesn't fry your brain, let me give you an analogy.

You would never embark on a trip without knowing where you're going. You identify the roads or freeways to take to get to your final destination.

Keywords, at their most basic, are a road map. The right keywords put you on a road to success; the wrong ones lead you to getting lost and stopping to ask a gas station attendant how to find the right highway.

The other element of keywords that's important to mention is that strings of keywords narrow your lane even further. Singular keywords get you on the right road, but keyword strings get you in the right lane, which will help your reader get to your book even faster. In a minute, we'll look at why this matters but for now, consider the last search you did on Google. Did you put in one keyword like "mystery" or "romance"? Likely not. You probably plugged in a string of keywords like "most romantic weekend getaways" or "best mystery dinner theaters." Google and Amazon searches both respond better to keyword strings than to single keywords.

Let's explore keywords strings so you have a better understanding of what they are.

KEYWORD STRING STRATEGIES FOR GREATER VISIBILITY

Several years ago Google found that the more keywords a consumer puts into a search bar, the closer he or she is to a buy, meaning that if you type in "hybrid car" on the Google search bar, you're maybe only 20% ready to buy. But if you type in "Toyota hybrid sedan," there's a good chance you'll have a new car in a few months.

This is why when you're searching for something and putting lots of search criteria into Google, you'll start to see ads for the thing you searched almost everywhere, including Facebook.

For this reason, when I talk about keywords, I'm always referring to keyword strings—several keywords that together form a more focused search and, in some cases, even small sentences.

The other reason keyword strings are better than individual keywords is that, by creating a more focused search, they help to narrow the competition. Instead of trying to compete with "romance," "food allergies," or "business books," you can create a more focused funnel so you're driving the exact right readers to your book.

Consider:

Food allergies in children

Food allergies in women
Romance and international mystery
Romance and secret baby
Starting a new business
Business ideas for millennials
You get the idea.

UNPACKING THE SIX KEYS TO AMAZON RANKING

In an earlier chapter, I mentioned that everything matters. Before we dig into the keywords, let's look at the specific areas that matter to Amazon ranking:

- Popularity of your genre
- Matching search terms
- Social proof/reviews
- Pricing strategy
- Book page
- Amazon ads

We're going to break down each of these subjects in this book, but let's spend a few minutes discussing the first bullet—popularity of your genre—because that can get tricky.

I can't tell you how many times I've spoken with authors who write a book that's "never been written." Don't get me wrong. I always love new ideas, but Amazon doesn't. Yes, there are always new ways to tell stories and new things to teach, but having a book that doesn't fall into a specific genre is a problem. In some cases, authors are just sitting in the wrong genre altogether, which impacts everything from search to relevancy score.

This book isn't about deciding whether your book has an audience or not; that should have been part of your research. But you absolutely should make sure that your book is sitting in the appropriate genre/category. We'll look more closely at that as we delve deeper into optimization, but for now it's worth mentioning that if your book isn't gaining any traction, it could be that the market is limited or that you're sitting in the wrong market altogether.

Despite the insane number of books on Amazon, you can still be on page one or claim the number one ranking.

That's because most people aren't aware that Amazon is its own search engine. But now you *are* aware, and you can use the information to your advantage. Keep in mind that the tools shared in this book won't guarantee your book will hit the number one spot on Amazon, but they will help you generate a significant amount of attention. In the end, isn't that what you want?

UNDERSTANDING AMAZON METADATA

There was a time when no one talked about metadata. Now it's a buzzword. But metadata means different things, depending on the website where you're planning to sell your book. Amazon differs from other sites, and it's important to know why:

The only things related to metadata that Amazon cares about are your keyword strings and your book's (enhanced) categories.

Zeroing in on Amazon's metadata is a fantastic way to generate more attention for your book, and the great thing is that everything counts. Your book title, subtitle, and keyword strings—everything matters, and I'll break this down throughout this book.

But first let's take a closer look at metadata, so you can see what I mean.

MAKING YOUR BOOK MORE SEARCHABLE

The more searchable your book is, the more often it's going to come up in searches, and consequently, the more books you'll sell.

Part of this is due to Amazon's metadata, which is available to all authors who have a book on Amazon, but most authors and publishers don't use it or understand it—not because they're lazy but because it's complex and ever-changing.

KDP, Amazon's Kindle Direct Publishing program and

Amazon's eBook arm, is a popular way to get your book onto the Amazon platform. But it isn't the only way to populate keyword strings in the Amazon system. If you've published through another service that allows you to populate keywords in your metadata, these will help you on the Amazon site as well because those keywords will get pushed through that system as well as any you set up directly on the KDP dashboard.

To keep this chapter simple, I'm going to focus on the KDP dashboard. Just know that everything you learn here can be applied to virtually any dashboard you publish on.

If you're traditionally published, this information will work, too. I'll show you how to do this search and hand the results over to your publisher.

If you've published on Amazon via KDP, the screenshot of the dashboard below probably looks familiar to you. This dashboard is where you access all of your books' metadata and the enhanced categories, which I'll explain shortly.

kindle direct publishing   Bookshelf   Reports   Community   Marketing

Paperback Details	Paperback Content	Paperback Rights & Pricing
✓ Complete	ⓘ Not Started...	ⓘ Not Started...

Language

Choose your paperback's primary language (the language in which the book was written). Learn more about languages supported for paperbacks.

English ⌄

Book Title

Enter your title as it appears on the book cover. This field cannot be changed after your book is published. Learn more about book titles.

Book Title

The Amazon Author Forumla

Keywords   Choose up to 7 keywords that describe your book. How do I choose keywords? ˅

Your Keywords (Optional)

You can see you're allowed up to seven search keywords, which should be keyword phrases, or strings.

Although Amazon says they're optional, they should *never* be optional nor overlooked. While I was doing research for this book, I asked 10 authors to let me take a look at the back-end, behind-the-scenes details of their books, with the caveat that I wouldn't add terms they didn't need. *None* of them had search words listed. All my authors had chosen their categories, but search keywords (and enhanced categories) are too often ignored.

We're going to dig into keyword string strategies in the next chapter, but for now just start percolating some ideas. No doubt, you also see from the above screenshot that I'm using keyword strings, *not* single keywords. Though we've covered that point, it's worth calling your attention to it again. Yes, it's that important.

THE REWARDS OF AN OPTIMIZED BOOK

In addition to the search engine side of Amazon, there is the store. As a retailer, Amazon's goal is to sell stuff, and a lot of it.

We'll talk in more depth about the retailer aspect later in this book, but what I've found is that most authors list their books on Amazon and think they're done. They just assume Amazon will do the selling for them. That couldn't be further from the truth. There are certain strategies you *must* implement before you can relax a bit.

Aside from being a great place to sell your book, Amazon can become an author's best friend with the application of a little bit of know-how.

In addition to the mysterious search engine component I will unravel for you shortly, there's also the brick-and-mortar sales model Amazon uses. This model is essentially a big piece of its algorithm.

Let's say you're the manager of a clothing store, and one day you notice your cashmere sweaters (last season's style) are selling. Normally you wouldn't put them at the front of your store, since you leave that area for the known hits—the most trending products, the ones you know will sell well. But when something you hadn't expected to sell starts gaining interest, you naturally figure it's a good idea to give it more exposure, and you put it a bit closer to the front.

Now the sweaters are selling even faster, and you move them to one of the front tables. Bingo! You sell even more. Then one day, when you're redoing your storefront window, you think, Let's display them here. Suddenly, your stock is sold out.

This is essentially what happens with Amazon, except replace the sweater with your book. When your book starts selling on Amazon, the superstore takes notice, and your book starts popping up in all sorts of places that relate to book recommendations.

If you own a Kindle, you know that when you're looking to buy a book or have just finished reading one, the system shows you other books on the same or similar topics. That is one of the many ways Amazon pushes a book that's selling or showing great promise.

Have you ever wished you could see your book there?

How exactly does it happen, and how can you make it work for you?

That's where the algorithm/search engine model and this book come into play. What I'll show you relates to algorithm triggers within Amazon's search function.

Almost 100% of the time, when I look at Amazon author profiles, I find that authors aren't doing much to promote their titles. In fact, many of your book promotion tasks require your own "marketing muscle." Much of that marketing muscle is actually marketing know-how—a skill with which most of us aren't born.

Regardless of when your book was published or whether the subject matter is still relevant, you can boost it on Amazon using these techniques. I've seen it happen with books that are five years old or even older. If you're wondering if you can make it work for your book, let me assure you, you can!

With the exception of Amazon ads, all the strategies I recommend in this book are free and will cost you only the time spent on research and tracking. As I mentioned earlier, some things I show you may produce immediate results; others will take a little time.

Once you implement these strategies, however, it's a bit of "set it and forget it," meaning that once you've done the heavy lifting, the algorithm kicks in and Amazon does the rest.

HOW TO RESEARCH KEYWORD STRINGS ON AMAZON

Just about everything we'll talk about ties back to your keyword strings, which is why I decided to dedicate a few chapters to unpacking this often-mysterious concept. You'll likely refer to this chapter often, since various strategies in the book will tie back to it.

The first thing you should know is that keyword strings on Amazon all fall under a basic economic principle: supply and demand. Put simply, we're aiming for very little supply for something that's in high demand.

This chapter will show you exactly how to do that.

GETTING STARTED

When you're starting out, finding keyword strings can seem like an arduous and complex task, but it doesn't have to be. I'll show you a few simple ways to build your keyword strings on Amazon. Carve out an hour or so to start building your list.

WHAT ABOUT USING SOFTWARE?

Generally, I'm opposed to keyword software because I always find that the searches on Amazon tend to be more accurate. However, I have used the Google Adword (Keyword) Planner as well as Uber-suggest.

The best keyword strings are ones you find manually. Why? With so many books being published on Amazon, it would be hard for any software—even Google's robust Keyword Planner—to give you 100% accurate results. Seeing the results with your own eyes is the only way to truly validate your choices. Also, keep in mind that sites like Ubersuggest and Google's Keyword Planner are based on search activity but don't take into account consumer preferences, which we'll dig into in this chapter. There's a big difference between what people are searching for and what they're actually buying.

Amazon Tip!
You're allowed up to seven keyword strings when you upload your book to Amazon's Kindle Direct Publishing (KDP). I suggest you come up with a minimum of 15 keyword strings while you're doing research, so you can swap them out and/or use them in your book description, product page blurbs, enhanced book description, or on your print book (if you're uploading it via KDP).

BUILDING IDEAS AND TESTING KEYWORDS

It always helps if you know the keywords and keyword strings your audience tends to use. If you don't know—which is often the case with nonfiction authors—you'll want to start by testing some keyword strings to find out what seems to work well for your book, subject matter, niche, or genre.

SEARCHING FOR GREAT KEYWORD STRINGS ON AMAZON

If you're doing a search on Amazon to find keyword strings for your book or books, I suggest starting on the Kindle side of the Amazon website.

Not every search is created equal; searching for "mystery and suspense" on the main Amazon site instead of specifically in the Kindle department will net you very different and largely inaccurate results.

And since so many books are eBooks only, the Kindle side of Amazon is denser than the print book side and yields a better representation of what you're really against.

Quick Search Tip!

Before you start, tee up an "incognito" search page. You don't want Amazon's preferences following your searches, and using an incognito page will help you examine authentic searches, compared to searches based on your prior activity on Amazon.

To begin your keyword string search, select Kindle Store from the dropdown (left-hand side of the search below), leaving the search bar blank, and click the orange search button (with the magnifying glass symbol).

Next, click Kindle eBooks.

Once you're there, start typing your keywords into the search bar. While you're keying them in, Amazon's intuitive search will start to drop down suggestions. Not all of the suggestions will be ones you'll use, but they're certainly a good start.

Here is what a dropdown might look like if you typed just the word "romance" into the Kindle search bar:

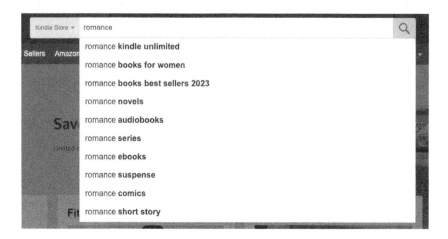

As these suggestions pop up, make a note of them or grab a screenshot as I did. We'll discuss vetting these in a minute. But first, let's dig deeper into the keyword must-haves. Ideally you want your keyword string to match the following criteria:

- It's worth mentioning this again: Use only keyword *strings*. Do not settle for single keywords because consumers don't search that way. You wouldn't Google with just the word "suspense," either.
- Don't assume Amazon's recommendations, such as those from the above screenshot, are the exact right ones for your book. In a minute, we'll look at how to determine that.

UNDERSTANDING AMAZON'S SALES RANK

It's a good time to discuss the mysteries behind Amazon's sales rank. This is the rank you see on the various retail book pages about halfway down the page. Under "Product Details," you'll see information such as publisher, book length, and Best Sellers Rank, which is what we're focused on now.

Amazon's book rankings go into the millions; the higher the number, the fewer books you're selling. The lower the number, the more you're selling.

Did You Know?
If your Best Sellers Rank is 27,000 or less, your book is considered to be in the top 1% of Amazon!

Many things can impact your sales rank. For example, if you just did a discounted eBook promotion, you'll no doubt see a pop in your sales rank, which will likely drop off once the promotion is over. Many authors see a pop in their Best Sellers Rank upon book launch, which is normal. But then it's likely to drop off as the book ages. We'll address your first 30 days on Amazon in a future chapter, but for now it's good to note your rank on Amazon.

Pro Tip for Miscategorized Books
If this chapter prompted you to look at your sales rank on Amazon and you found out your book is showing up under the wrong category, don't panic. For example, you have a women's fiction book that seems to be trending under mysteries or paranormal; that means that you haven't done your

optimization. Something in your keywords is driving your book
to the wrong category on Amazon. This book will help you fix
that!

There are numerous blog posts about understanding sales rank so you can gauge how well a book is selling based on the rank. The issue with this view is it's not entirely accurate. Why? Because your book's sales rank can also be impacted by visitors to your page. For example, if you're running a BookBub promotion and you see your sales rank soaring but your sales aren't matching that, it means that you sent a lot of traffic to your page but only a fraction of visitors bought the book.

The other reason guessing at sales is not a good idea is that, with 8,216 books published each day in this country and many of them winding up on Amazon, the sales ranks can fluctuate wildly.

Why then am I pushing you to look for books with a low sales rank if that doesn't always mean the book is selling? A low sales rank means there's lots of attention to that title and, very likely, it's selling well. Certainly, it's showing up in great searches and getting traffic. That's why the rank matters.

TAKING IT STEP BY STEP

Let's go to the next step and break this down even further. Say you have a book about creating a home office or building a business from home. I'd start with the keyword string "working from home." You'll notice from the screenshot below that the number of books in that particular search term is only 2,000, meaning there is a relatively low number of books on that topic. Considering that there are eight million books on Amazon (and growing daily), 2,000 books is a reasonably low number. In terms of "supply," we're in a good place. Next we're going to check the demand for this keyword string.

It's important to note here that the search has turned up a list of books that are somewhat older, which does not impact the integrity of the keyword string. Next, I'm going to click on the first three books to check their sales ranks. To do this, click on the book and scroll down to "Product Details."

Product details

ASIN : B071CTK28D

Publisher : Simon & Schuster; Illustrated edition (September 19, 2017)

Publication date : September 19, 2017

Language : English

File size : 14584 KB

Text-to-Speech : Enabled

Screen Reader : Supported

Enhanced typesetting : Enabled

X-Ray : Enabled

Word Wise : Enabled

Print length : 593 pages

Lending : Not Enabled

Best Sellers Rank: #9,341 in Kindle Store (See Top 100 in Kindle Store)
  #7 in Investing Basics
  #13 in Personal Success in Business
  #15 in Business Leadership

Customer Reviews: ★★★★½ ˅   11,999 ratings

To reiterate the point about aged books vs. new ones, as I clicked through these books, I discovered age wasn't a factor in their success. They all seemed to be doing well. Sales rankings were low, a solid indicator that we now have a keyword string that meets the right criteria: low supply, high demand. You'll want to do this several more times until you have all the keyword strings you'll need.

WHAT IF YOU CAN'T FIND A LOW SALES RANK?

Sales rank indicates a book's sales in relation to other books' sales. A book ranked number one has in theory sold the most. A large number on the sales rank line isn't good. A book ranking of 88,453 means that 88,452 books are selling better than this book. A great rank is normally 10,000 or less.

But this ranking also depends to some degree on the genre, niche, or subject matter. For example, a sales rank of 13,000 may not seem strong. But for some of my own nonfiction books, that number means they're selling pretty well. In some cases (and because I write non-fiction), I'm doing $500-plus in book sales per month at that sales rank. However, when I look at that 13,000 rank in fiction, the sales are often lower.

The same is true for an author who publishes in a very crowded genre like mystery, romance, or YA. You might be hoping for a low sales rank but you're only finding books with sales ranks of 25,000 and above.

Part of the issue could be the keyword string, but it could also be that the genre is crowded and competitive. My recommendation is give it a shot. Grab those keywords even if they aren't ideal and see if you get some bounce from them. If you don't, then head back to the drawing board for more ideas.

The other issue you may encounter is the number of books under a particular keyword string (the supply number).

Let's say you have a royal romance book, so you go onto Amazon and type in "royal romance." The keyword string shows a relatively low number of books, considering the popularity of the genre. (As of this writing I'm showing around 10,000. You might want to verify this along with me. It's good practice!)

While 10,000 may seem high, consider how crowded the genre is. Also, it's interesting to note that in the last edition of this book (updated a year ago), that number was just 6,000!

Romance of any kind is a heavily populated category, so I went with this keyword string and checked the sales rank of the titles. I was pleasantly surprised by what I found. Each of the books under that particular search string had a fairly low sales rank.

THE SURPRISING IMPORTANCE OF MANUAL SEARCHES

All of this seems like a great deal of work, doesn't it? I'm not going to lie; there's some work involved, but I promise you it's absolutely worth doing these searches manually and here's why.

Why Popular keywords aren't always selling books

As you start searching for keywords, it's important to understand that beyond being a popular search term on Amazon, the ideal keyword string also leads you to books that are selling well. This is called a "funnel." Surprisingly, even some keyword strings that rank high on Amazon are not terrific funnels. Why? Because although they may be searched frequently, they might not have the types of books your consumer wants. In other words, for whatever reason, consumers aren't buying the books that show up on these searches.

Often this happens when books are populated to a category that doesn't have heavy traffic. The suggestions that pop up on Amazon are based on frequent *searches*, not sales. Suggested search strings don't necessarily mean they have a high enough frequency of search or enough buyers looking at that category to boost your book sales. It simply means the string is being searched often enough to be noticed and included in an algorithm.

Flipping Your Keywords

Sometimes keywords need to be flipped. For example, you might have what you feel is a sure thing, like "time travel and romance." I did this search, and I was surprised to find that the keyword string wasn't really getting a lot of traction. When I flipped it to "romance and time travel," the search results were much better.

If you're not sure, experiment with flipping the keywords.

Digging Deeper into Supply and Demand

The general rule about supply and demand comes with a few exceptions. You may find a keyword string with a small number of books in it, but checking the sales rank makes you second-guess your options because the sales rank number is very large (meaning the book isn't selling a lot of copies). This can happen with some keyword strings. Some may have a small number of books, but the sales rank number on the books is pretty high, generally in the hundreds of thousands. This means there is a small number of books under that search term, but it also means they aren't selling.

The flip side of this is when you think, "Okay, I'll put my book in there and get to the number one spot with little or no effort."

I thought that too, and I shifted a romance book into a narrow keyword string. The book dropped dramatically in the rankings, which points us back to this key factor: even if Amazon suggests the keyword string, you still need to do your own homework to make sure it's the right choice for you.

MORE UNIQUE WAYS TO SEARCH

If you've tried to find something on Google, you have most likely used a search string that involves the word "and." For example, you entered "mystery and book" or something along those lines. The same type of search string works on Amazon, but there's a bit of a twist to it. Let me show you what I mean.

Let's say you wrote a romance novel, and you're trying to find out what your potential readers are searching for. Head over to Amazon and type in "romance and," and see what pops up:

These are autosuggestions based on your keyword plus the word "and." Let's take this a step further and add the beginning of another word, creating a search string that looks like this: "Romance and s." Take a look at the screenshot below:

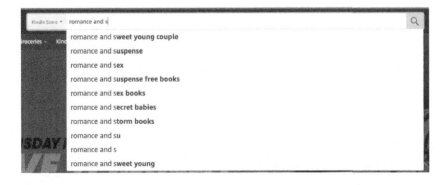

It brings up more search suggestions—and possible ideas for more keywords.

Although it doesn't typically happen in fiction as much as it does in nonfiction, it's still a good idea to remember that certain keyword strings change seasonally. Seasonal tie-ins to your topic should be factored into the keyword string *only as long as that string is getting enough searches.*

With nonfiction you can see changes in searches based on what's going on in the news or major shifts in industry trends. If you're an expert on your topic and you're keeping up with what's happening in your industry, you could benefit from doing keyword research to see if searches on Amazon have shifted in a way you can take advantage of as well.

Now you know a little more about the different ways to search for optimal keyword strings. Depending on your subject, genre, or niche, you may want to try them all. But remember, if you decide to change your keyword strings, be sure to add them to your book description, and maybe even incorporate them in your title if your book's not "on the shelves" yet.

Now you've learned the tools for searching keyword strings and how to use them. You can use your knowledge on many levels while you get ready to publish a book that will sell, or market a book that isn't selling well—yet.

SIMPLE KEYWORD STRING SUCCESS STRATEGIES TO ROCK YOUR BOOK

Before we dive deeper into optimization and dig into categories, let's look at some creative ways to use keywords.

Now that you understand where your keyword strings come into play in the context of your Amazon back-end, behind-the-scenes information, it's a good time to explore other ways a strategic set of keywords can help you on the front end.

TITLES AND SUBTITLES

Regardless of the genre you've written in, your book title should be benefit-driven. In fact, a book's title can often make or break its success, but most authors fail to consider adding keyword strings to their title and/or subtitle. And while keywords in a title are very particular to nonfiction, anyone can use a subtitle on their Amazon retail page.

Many times, particularly in nonfiction, I see authors give their books nebulous titles. This is a mistake, especially when you consider all the titles on Amazon and all the books your reader has to choose from. If you've written nonfiction, be as benefit-driven and as specific as you can be. If you've written fiction, create a title that isn't hard to pronounce, isn't too long, and will appeal to your reader.

At this point, some of you are probably thinking you've missed the boat because your book is already out, but you haven't!

Whether or not you've already published your book, there are some key strategies pertaining to subtitles that can benefit you.

If you've written nonfiction and your book has a subtitle on the cover, you'll have to go with that subtitle. But if you don't have a subtitle on the cover, here's your chance to add it to your Amazon book page.

Check out these books. Both have great subtitles that have been added to their book page:

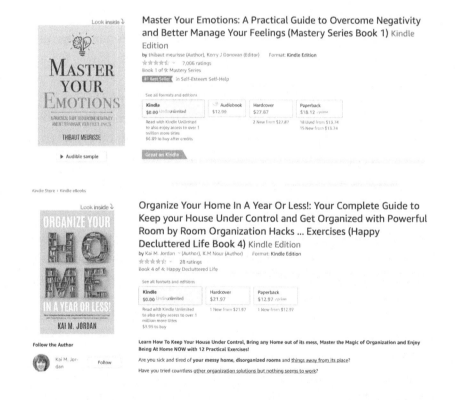

In the case of the home organization book, I might have edited that subtitle down slightly because very long subtitles make the page look heavy and are harder to focus on. But this gives you an idea of what I'm talking about.

Amazon Tip!
If you have a nonfiction book out with a not-so-great subtitle, consider redoing the cover to include a fresh, new, keyword-driven subtitle and uploading it to Amazon to replace your current cover. Then you have an eye-popping subtitle you can use on your retail page.

USING DESCRIPTIVE SUBTITLES IN FICTION

Some fiction books put their descriptive subtitles right on the cover. That means the authors did their research in advance and knew what their dramatic hook was when their cover was being created. But most of the authors I've worked with don't focus on adding a descriptive subtitle to their cover and instead just add it to the Amazon book page.

You can also create a descriptive subtitle after your book cover has been designed by simply adding a subtitle on the back end of Amazon. Here's an example of a great subtitle that isn't listed on the book's cover.

Subtitles help to differentiate your book on search pages, too. Check out the same book on the Amazon search page:

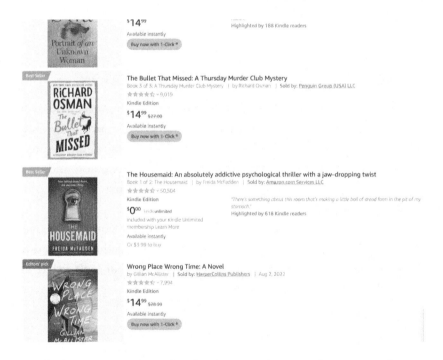

These subtitles give the books an effective descriptive boost. With so many elements on Amazon intended to distract readers and draw their attention to other products, it's smart to assume readers no longer spend a lot of time reading book descriptions, and vague "guess what this book is about" book titles just don't work anymore. Now the majority of browsing time is spent with the cover image, title, and subtitle. You can see how the subtitle above further enhances the page while also speaking to the reader's particular goal in finding the right book.

YOUR BOOK DESCRIPTION

Later in this book I've dedicated an entire chapter to your Amazon book page, but if you're ready to dig into this, head on over there now.

UNDERSTANDING AMAZON ENHANCED CATEGORIES

Your book categories are like lanes on a highway, driving traffic to (or in some cases away from) your book. And this is why they're so critically important. The wrong categories can actually hurt your book, while the exact right categories can drive lots and lots of eyes to your Amazon book page. But categories are so much more than simply where your audience will find your book. The more niched, the more specific you can get, the better. This is why I refer to categories as "enhanced."

The reality is this: the narrower your category, the better you'll do on Amazon overall. Much of this has to do with the way the algorithm works. Some nonfiction authors look at bigger categories, like business or self-help, and think, I want to dominate that category! That is a great goal, but it's often not realistic. Dominating a smaller niche category will trigger Amazon algorithms, which in turn trigger more visibility for your book.

On Amazon, sales breed sales. The more sales you get, the more sales Amazon wants you to get. Digging into niche categories can be another way to trigger this sales-focused algorithm.

DISSECTING THE AMAZON WEBSITE

The Amazon website is actually a bunch of sites under one umbrella, and the algorithms for each of these sites all have different markers. Let me explain.

You'd never start searching for a book under the Whole Foods site on Amazon because that would bring up a bunch of odd search suggestions; the same is true for the Amazon Handmade site. Each of these subsets of the Amazon site responds differently to searches. The book site is also divided into two sites: the print book side and the Kindle side. And it absolutely does matter to your search results.

If you're doing category research only on the main book site, you may be missing out on some great possibilities. My preference is to do category research only in the Amazon Kindle store. Why? Since so many of the new books being published on Amazon are published exclusively to the Kindle format, the Kindle side is weightier in terms of search results. You'll also get a better variety of suggestions and enhancements.

A while back Amazon also changed how many categories any book can have. Originally you were allowed to have four, then Amazon dropped it to two. For a long time you were allowed to have ten categories. But in typical Amazon style, that changed too. In June of 2023, Amazon limited book categories to three. That is unfortunate, but the good news is that the enhanced categories I'm addressing in this book still work. You're just limited to three.

Even with only three categories, you'll want to have a mix of niche categories and broader ones. Yes, niche categories are a must. And if you have three niche categories, great; stick with that. But every genre is different in terms of how deep and unique these enhanced categories get. When you're trying to decide which categories make the most sense, it helps to think outside your core market. For example, if you've written a business or nutrition book, instead of leaving the book in "Business" or "Dieting," two very crowded categories on Amazon, put it into something slightly narrower, like the subcategory "Women and Business" or "Macrobiotics," to help make sure it won't get lost. I'll address these subcategories again shortly, in more depth.

You may also want to mix up your markets and consider other areas your book might do well in. For example, I have a book called *Red Hot Internet Publicity*, which I put in both the "Business" and "Internet Marketing" sections. Readers might search both areas, so I'm covered.

Be aware that categories can change and often do—sometimes without notice. Sometimes Amazon even deletes categories. It won't delete your book from the system, but it will delete it from that category and arbitrarily put it somewhere else.

Note to Authors Published on the Kindle Direct Publishing (KDP) Platform

If you're a KDP author, you'll select your categories on the KDP portal, rather than emailing the KDP staff to have them changed. If you've read any previous editions of this book, you know that I recommended finding your categories and then emailing Amazon's KDP team to change your categories. Amazon has done away with that. All category changes are done on the back end, via the KDP site where you upload your eBook. The categories in the KDP dashboard still mirror the enhanced and niche categories on Amazon, so I recommend finding those categories first and then matching them up with the categories in your KDP portal.

FINDING THE BEST CATEGORIES ON AMAZON

The Kindle side of Amazon has some great additional categories for your book. Here's how to access it:

- Go to the Amazon.com search bar and highlight Kindle Store (as we previously discussed).
- Then click the magnifying glass but don't put a book title in the search bar. Highlighting Kindle Store and clicking Go will drop you into the Kindle side of Amazon, which has a completely different set of categories.
- Once you're there, click on Categories at the top, and voilà, you can really start digging around. The key is to keep clicking that bar to the left (see image below) until you find some good categories in which to put your book.

< Kindle Store

Kindle eBooks

Arts & Photography

Biographies & Memoirs

Business & Money

Children's eBooks

Comics, Manga & Graphic Novels

Computers & Technology

Cookbooks, Food & Wine

Crafts, Hobbies & Home

Education & Teaching

Engineering & Transportation

Foreign Languages

Health, Fitness & Dieting

History

Humor & Entertainment

Law

LGBTQ+ eBooks

Literature & Fiction

Medical eBooks

Mystery, Thriller & Suspense

Nonfiction

Parenting & Relationships

Politics & Social Sciences

Reference

Religion & Spirituality

Romance

Science & Math

Science Fiction & Fantasy

Self-Help

Sports & Outdoors

Teen & Young Adult

Travel

Let's be clear: you are on the eBook side of Amazon. I'll talk more about that in a moment because when you or your publisher uploaded your book to Amazon, you probably picked some industry standard categories, called BISAC categories. These are going to be vastly different, but for now let's dig deeper into finding some great pathways for your book!

Let's say you have a book about dieting, if I click on "Health, Fitness & Dieting," I get this dropdown:

< Kindle eBooks

Health, Fitness & Dieting

Addiction & Recovery

Alternative Medicine

Beauty, Grooming, & Style

Counseling & Psychology

Death & Grief

Diets & Weight Loss

Diseases & Physical Ailments

Exercise & Fitness

Nutrition

Personal Health

Reference

Relationships

Safety & First Aid

Sex

Sports Health & Safety

Teen Health

Let's click on "Counseling & Psychology" and see what we get:

< Health, Fitness & Dieting

Counseling & Psychology

Adolescent Psychology

Applied Psychology

Child Development & Psychology

Clinical Psychology

Cognitive Neuroscience & Cognitive Neuropsychology

Counseling

Creativity & Genius

Developmental Psychology

Education & Training

Essays

Ethnopsychology

Evolutionary Psychology

Experimental Psychology

Forensic Psychology

Grief & Loss

Group Therapy

History

Human Sexuality

Hypnosis

Medicine & Psychology

Mental Health

Movements

Neuropsychology

Occupational & Organizational

Pathologies

Personality

Physiological Aspects

Practice Management

Psychoanalysis

Psychopharmacology

Psychotherapy, TA & NLP

Look at all of the options you have! These are all terrific options to categorize your book. And sometimes if you click on these options, more drop-down options appear for even more niche categories. It doesn't happen for each genre or subgenre, but sometimes you get lucky and can go pretty far into your niche.

Now let's look at fiction.

I've clicked on "Mystery, Thriller & Suspense," and look at all of the options here.

‹ Kindle eBooks

Mystery, Thriller & Suspense

Crime Fiction

Mystery

Science Fiction

Suspense

Thrillers

The same is true for literature and fiction:

< Kindle eBooks

Literature & Fiction

Absurdist

Action & Adventure

Adaptations & Pastiche

Animals

Anthologies & Literature Collections

Black & African American

British

Classics

Contemporary Fiction

Drama & Plays

Erotica

Essays & Correspondence

Foreign Language Fiction

Genre Fiction

Historical Fiction

Horror

Humor & Satire

Literary Criticism

Literary Fiction

Mythology & Folk Tales

People with Disabilities

Poetry

Religious & Inspirational Fiction

Short Stories

Small Town & Rural

United States

Women's Fiction

World Literature

Now let's zero in on women's fiction, a popular genre. When I click on it, look at all the possible choices:

< Literature & Fiction

Women's Fiction

Action & Adventure

Black & African American

Christian

Contemporary

Fantasy

Historical

Humor

Lesbian

Literary

Mystery, Thriller & Suspense

New Adult & College

Psychological

Religious

Romance

Sagas

Short Stories

Women's Poetry

As you can see, there are many options under this drop-down, too. Let's say you have a mystery book or a romance novel; you might want to add this to your list of categories.

This is why it makes sense to play with this a bit. Really click down to find some great and narrow categories.

The Dead End Categories on Amazon

Ever since Amazon made their recent category changes, it's been noted that not all of the categories you may pick on the backend of Amazon are actually categories. Some of these just run to deadend pages. So what does this mean for you and how can you avoid this happening to your book?

Well, you need to have your book tethered to a category that *is* an actual category, not one that runs to a blank page because that won't serve you at all. For this reason, you really want to do your category research on the front end of Amazon, not while you're uploading your book to the platform. When you select your category from the Amazon website directly, you know it's a viable, working category, too.

This may change by the time this book is published – because Amazon is an ever-changing ecosystem – but it was worth mentioning and alerting you, in case the issue still exists.

CHANGING YOUR CATEGORIES ON AMAZON

When you first publish on Amazon or add your book (and eBook) to its system, you're asked for the categories where you want your book listed. As I mentioned earlier, these are your standard industry categories, called BISAC, used by everyone from bookstores to specialty stores. The categories I'm suggesting here are eBook-specific, but they will benefit you nonetheless. Your categories for your eBook will be different, and we'll discuss those in a minute.

When you've found the right category for your eBook in the Kindle store, make sure your book is added to it. If you're with a traditional publisher, ask your editor or marketer to move your book into these enhanced categories. But if you're published via

KDP, just make the changes on the back end of the Kindle Direct Publishing portal as I mentioned earlier. If you're with a publisher, you can send your contact the categories you've identified and ask the publisher to make the changes from its portal.

WHY REFINE-BY THEMES MATTER FOR FICTION

What are refine-by themes?

Refine-by themes are, in general, various aspects of your book's content. For example, if you have a wealthy protagonist, one of your themes would be "Wealthy." If you have a murder mystery with a serial killer, your theme might be "Serial Killer."

Amazon implemented its refine-by section for fiction because consumers were searching for particular traits such the type of protagonist or setting (beach, city, etc.).

Here's what themes look like on the romance side of the Amazon page:

Romantic Heroes

- [ ] Alpha Males
- [ ] BBW
- [ ] Bikers
- [ ] Cowboys
- [ ] Criminals & Outlaws
- [ ] Doctors
- [ ] Firefighters
- [ ] Highlanders
- [ ] Pirates
- [ ] Royalty & Aristocrats
- [ ] Spies
- [ ] Vikings
- [ ] Wealthy

Romantic Themes

- [ ] Amnesia
- [ ] Beaches
- [ ] International
- [ ] Love Triangle
- [ ] Medical
- [ ] Second Chances
- [ ] Secret Baby
- [ ] Vacation
- [ ] Wedding
- [ ] Workplace

You can see a list of "Romantic Heroes" and "Romantic Themes" on the left-hand side of the screen. If you've written a thriller or mystery, you'll have three choices: "Moods & Themes," "Characters," and "Settings."

Moods & Themes

- [ ] Action-packed
- [ ] Dark
- [ ] Disturbing
- [ ] Fun
- [ ] Gory
- [ ] Humorous
- [ ] Racy & Risque
- [ ] Romantic
- [ ] Scary
- [ ] Vengeful

Characters

- [ ] Amateur Sleuths
- [ ] British Detectives
- [ ] Gay Protagonists
- [ ] FBI Agents
- [ ] Female Protagonists
- [ ] Lesbian Protagonists
- [ ] Police Officers
- [ ] Private Investigators

Settings

- [ ] Beaches
- [ ] Islands
- [ ] Mountains
- [ ] Outer Space
- [ ] Small Towns
- [ ] Suburban
- [ ] Urban

How do you use refine-by themes in your Amazon strategy?

First, it's good to know what consumers are searching for. As you're pulling together keywords, be aware of these bigger subsets of searches. You can use these keywords in your Amazon keywords and in your book description. An Amazon rep told me that for a book to be found under a particular search—e.g., "female protagonists"—the phrase needs to be somewhere in your keyword string. So, your keyword string might be "female protagonist international thriller."

Test adding refine-by keywords to your other keyword strings. Qualify them the same way you do other keywords, by checking their supply and demand. Not all of them will work, mind you. Some are just too specific and, while readers are interested in books in these niche categories, if they're not using those exact words in searches, the words won't help you. However, some refine-bys are easy to incorporate and often produce positive results—like adding "dark" to an already solid keyword string for a thriller or suspense book. Take advantage of these easy wins.

PART TWO
YOUR AMAZON
BOOK PAGE

CREATIVE WAYS TO ACHIEVE MORE VISIBILITY FOR YOUR BOOK ON AMAZON

O f all the things authors struggle with, pinpointing exactly how their book can benefit the reader is one of the trickiest. Highlighting your book benefits—aka the benefits to the reader—is the single most important step you can take to make your book stand out, not just on Amazon but everywhere you're promoting it.

Defining and refining your book's benefits isn't easy and, though this is particularly important for nonfiction, I'm going to tether fiction authors to this in a minute.

For now, let's talk about the steam mop. Ever heard of it?

You may want to get one—unless you want to keep cleaning your floors with a regular mop that doesn't kill germs. Who wants that? Did you know you can also clean carpets and rugs with a steam mop?

See what I did there? I got you to go from "What the heck is a steam mop?" to "Well, yeah, I want to keep my floors germ-free!"

The idea is that you need **alignment**, and that's where your keyword strings (and your book description) can take you. Alignment is the concept of bringing together two ideas that aren't obviously related and then connecting them to sell your idea—in this case, your book.

First you need to find out "where it hurts." Identify the problem that needs to be solved.

Recently I was doing an Amazon optimization for a book about better breathing, in other words, how to oxygenate your blood better. This is an interesting market because it affects everyone. We all breathe. But it's also deceptive because most people don't head over to Amazon to learn how to breathe better. The upside for an author is that there aren't a lot of breathing books on Amazon.

Reduced competition sounds great, right? In reality, yes, but when it comes to Amazon, that could be problematic. The books about breathing already on Amazon all had high sales ranks, which means they aren't selling well, or there's no interest in learning how to breathe. But it's possible there's no interest in breathing books because the authors haven't connected the dots for the consumer.

While I was working on this optimization, I decided to go after different reasons someone might buy this book; for example, if you're feeling tired, or you suffer from brain fog, a book about breathing better could be helpful. The same is true for losing weight; somewhat surprising is that better breathing can also help with weight loss. The end result was a set of keyword strings that tied the book to those issues. Once we did that, the author was able to boost the overall ranking of the book on Amazon and get it in front of readers who might want to consider other options for dealing with fatigue, weight loss, memory, brain fog—the list is endless.

For this strategy to work, you need to make sure your book description matches and aligns with this train of thought. In the case of the breathing book, I suggested the author update the book description to include these benefits of better breathing, which matched the keywords and categories I found.

I followed the same process with a memoir of a husband's suicide due to a drug addiction. Memoirs are generally a tougher market, so I always try to anchor them to a bigger, broader message. In general, suicide is a tough subject to market. However, drug addiction is a massive problem in this country and, sadly, a topic many people can relate to, so that's where I focused my optimization efforts. I found channels, along with memoir and suicide, that the book would fit into and could also pull in readers who had dealt with addiction in a family member.

The goal in a category with low competition is a lower sales ranking, which translates to selling a ton of books, which is golden!

Additionally, I recommended that this author remove all references to death and suicide from her keyword strings and instead focus on addiction, drug addiction, memoir, and the like because suicide isn't heavily searched on Amazon. Remember, you want to align your book with the underlying factors for the outcome.

The same is true for fiction; regardless of your genre, it's all got to be benefit-driven. Adding things that drive a reader's interest, such as the setting (small-town romance, sweet romance) or the underlying theme (paranormal thriller), can all help to tether your book to something the reader wants. While this approach ties back to your keywords, it's also a good reminder, before we tackle maximizing your Amazon book page, that you have to make the connections for the readers. If you make them guess, you've lost a sale.

It's essential to make your book the end of the road in terms of readers' needs. Show them that whether they want to be entertained, educated, or enlightened, your book is what they need.

For most authors, this is where the book positioning gets derailed. They overlook this piece of it and/or make choices that are too broad, therefore losing opportunities for readers to find them.

If you can strategically position your book to match the benefits the reader is looking for (and even ones they hadn't considered, like the breathing book), you can present your book without a huge crowd of competing distractions and gain new readers. You'll be surprised how well this approach works.

GREAT AMAZON BOOK DESCRIPTIONS HELP SELL MORE BOOKS

Whether we're talking about Amazon or any other online retailer, book descriptions are more important than most authors realize.

Too often I see simple details overlooked that can make or break an author's ability to turn an Amazon browser into the next book buyer.

In this section, we'll discuss some ideas about book descriptions specifically, and then review some tips to enhance your own book description for maximum effectiveness on Amazon.

DUMB IT DOWN FOR BIGGER SALES

Most people bristle at the saying "dumb it down," but dumbing it down doesn't mean your audience is stupid; it means you're making your content easier to absorb. Brains are meant to conserve energy, and reading long, complex text exhausts the brain and consequently your target reader.

In his book, *The Bezos Blueprint*, author Carmine Gallo talks about why writing for an eighth-grade education level is key to appealing to a wider audience. Jeff Bezos is known for doing this in his speeches and yearly letters to his board. Fewer words, shorter sentences. He cites this statistic: Content written at the eight-grade level can be read and understood by 80% of Americans.

Using eighth-grade writing doesn't mean you sound like an eighth-grader; it simply denotes the amount of mental energy a consumer needs to use to absorb what you're telling them, i.e., your book description.

SCANNING VS. READING

Most people don't read websites; they scan them. The same is true for your book description. If you have huge blocks of text without any consideration for spacing, boldface type, bulleted lists, short paragraphs, or other forms of highlighting that help the reader scan and zero in on the best of the best you have to offer, that's unlikely to attract readers. When your description is visually and psychologically appealing, it invites the reader to keep going, instead of clicking to a different page.

Good book design follows this same methodology (which is why you never want to design your own book interior). The font on the pages should be visually appealing. By having wide margins (referred to as gutters in the book design world) and spacing, and in nonfiction, bulleted lists and boxed-in pieces to highlight particular text, you encourage the reader to take in all of your content, instead of doing a quick scan and rushing on.

Our minds are image processors, not text processors, so huge pieces of text that fill a page overwhelm the mind and in fact slow down the processing time considerably.

When we're looking at websites, our attention span is even shorter than it is when we're reading a book. Even on sites like Amazon—where consumers go to buy, and often spend a lot of time comparing products and reading reviews—it's important to keep in mind that most potential readers will move on if your description is too cumbersome.

THE Z-FACTOR ON YOUR AMAZON BOOK PAGE

There is nothing accidental about Amazon book pages (or any retail page on Amazon), the design and placement of all the elements is intentional. Even the Buy button is on the right-hand side for a reason.

Consumers surf in a Z fashion. Let's consider the Amazon book page for a moment:

Imagine the Z over this page: the eye starts with the cover, scans the title and rests on the Buy Now button (or in the case of the Kindle Unlimited, the Buy Now with 1-Click just underneath).

So, what does this mean to you? Although your book description is important, consumers don't see that first. They see your cover, book title, and Buy button in that order.

As we dig further into your Amazon retail page, you'll see the emphasis on a good subtitle for your book and book description, but if your cover is lackluster, you've probably already lost the sale and your buyer is off to find a book that appeals to him or her.

MAKING YOUR DESCRIPTION MORE SCAN-FRIENDLY

- **Headlines**: The first sentence in the description should be a grabber. Often, this is where authors use their elevator pitches (which we'll talk about in the next chapter). This text could also be an excerpt of an enthusiastic review or some other endorsement; regardless, it should be bolded, and your elevator pitch should always follow this format.

- **Paragraphs**: Keep paragraphs short, two to three sentences max, and let some powerful sentences stand on their own.
- **Bolding and Italics**: You can boldface key text throughout the description. In fact, I recommend it. Just don't use boldface or italics too much. It'll have more impact if you do just one sentence or a few keyword strings.
- **Bullets or Numbers**: If your book is nonfiction, it can be effective to bullet or number as much information as possible. Take key points and the "here's what you'll learn" elements and put them into a bulleted or numbered section that's easy to scan and visually appealing.

ANSWERING "WHAT'S IN IT FOR ME?"

The biggest challenge authors face is writing a book description that effectively highlights the book's benefits for readers. This matters for both fiction and nonfiction, and it's a crucial part of any book description.

Remember, with 8,200-plus books published *every day* in this country, you can't afford to have a vague, meandering book description. You must state clearly why your book is the best one readers can buy.

This leads us to the differences between fiction and nonfiction when it comes to book descriptions.

Nonfiction

First off, it's likely that whomever you're targeting already owns a few titles similar to the one you just published. Why should they add yours to their collection?

While you're powering through your book description, keep in mind that you're likely serving a cluttered market. Yes, you should feel confident you have a unique point of view, but potential readers won't know that if your book description isn't doing its job.

You need to be precise and clear about why your book matters. Hook the reader from the first sentence and make a personal connection via the book description.

Nonfiction shoppers are usually looking for the solution to a problem. They're not browsing for their next beach read, so your book description needs to *zero in on that particular problem.* Also, readers need to feel like you understand them and be convinced you're the best person to help them work through their problem.

If you're a noted expert in your field, with accolades to back up your reputation, work those in briefly, because praise does set you apart. Use reviews by other experts in your field or industry, but keep them short and sweet. Excerpts that highlight the plaudits should be used. Save your full bio and complete reviews for the other sections Amazon gives you. Some of the other sections are Editorial Reviews, About the Author, From the Author, From the Inside Flap, and From the Back Cover.

Fiction

Fiction is a bit tougher because it's easy to reveal too much or not quite enough. For this reason, I encourage you to focus on developing your elevator pitch because that's going to be your cliffhanger, or your readers' key interest point in the book. Every other piece of the story anchors to that.

When it comes to fiction, buyers have a lot of options, so be clear as to what your book is about and lead with the hook. Your opening sentence should be the best you've got; it might be the only chance you get. Don't confuse not giving it all away with being vague. If you're vague, you can't convince potential readers your book fits the genre they're interested in. They won't experience the emotional connection that makes them want to know more. Give them a story arc to latch onto that will leave them wanting more.

Keep movie trailers in mind while you're writing your fiction description. They often do an outstanding job of revealing enough of the story to get readers hooked without bogging them down with details they can't appreciate yet, or without revealing so much that it prevents them from watching it.

Children's and/or Young Adult Titles

For these books, make sure to include the intended age range. Even though you can add it in the Amazon details, I've had parents tell me that seeing the range in the book description is helpful because if anyone is short on time and needs help making smart buying decisions, it's parents.

It also helps to let them know right away what their child will learn, or what discussions or themes the book will highlight. You wrote the book for children, but you're selling it to adults, so don't oversimplify your description, thinking you're off the hook. Adjust your approach to reach parents who are short on time. They'll buy the book that leaves very little room for error, the book that seems like a sure thing.

WHY SIMPLE WORDING IS YOUR KEY TO SUCCESS

I've mentioned this previously, but it's worth repeating. When it comes to writing a book description, save your five-dollar words for another time. Book descriptions that work well tend to use simple language anyone can understand. If you make people pause to think about a word, you'll lose them.

Don't underestimate the power of a thesaurus. While you may want to repeat a few lucrative keyword strings, you don't want too much repetition because it will get boring. Great public speakers don't use the same words over and over because they understand the importance of creating effective sound bites, and they're smart about choosing words that aren't overused. This is a winning strategy for creating something memorable that stands out from the competition.

HOW EXCITED ARE YOU? AND HOW EXCITED WILL YOUR READERS BE?

Have you ever seen a book description with a ton of exclamation points or all caps? It probably feels as if the writer is screaming at you. Although I don't recommend eliminating exclamation points entirely from your book description, they should be used sparingly. I'd recommend one or two at most. An exclamation point here and there can help make a sentence seem more emphatic.

As far as all caps, don't even bother. Using all caps, even for a word or two or a single sentence in a book description, makes you look like an amateur.

THE ALL-IMPORTANT SPELL-CHECK

Using spell-check should be obvious for all authors, but I've seen enough descriptions loaded with typos that I feel like I need to say it. Please don't put up a book description full of typos. Even one typo is too many. Have a friend or colleague read your description before you put it on Amazon and again as soon as it's live. If necessary, make corrections ASAP.

SERIES AUTHORS, TAKE NOTE!

Fiction readers love a series. Tell them immediately that your book is part of an ongoing story or theme. Many readers are specifically searching for a great series when they come to Amazon. Include it in the headline. I recommend that you make it part of the title too. For example, you might word your book title like this: *Deadly Heat: Heat Series, Book 4 of 7.*

However, if your book is part of a series, new readers may not know whether they need to read them in order. The wording here is tricky for authors. If the books can be read out of order, you don't want to discourage new readers who may land on book 7 in your series and wonder if they have to invest their time to read through the six previous books before they can move onto book 7. It's a tough call for authors. When I ask series authors if their books can be read out of order, I find there's a lot of hesitation. "I'd prefer they read them in order." Yes, I agree; all series authors want this. But be honest with yourself: do the books *really* have to be read in order? If they can be read in any order, you don't want to miss out on potential sales.

If the books are stand-alone stories, mention that early in the book description to encourage, rather than discourage, new readers.

INCLUDE TOP KEYWORD STRINGS

Keywords are as important to your Amazon book page as almost anything else we've discussed. Using keywords is pretty easy if you're a nonfiction author, so for this section, we'll break this down for fiction authors.

Let's start by looking at two keyword strings. "Romance about second chances" and "Second-chance romances" have been popular search strings on Amazon for a while now. However, by taking those phrases and inserting them into your book description, you can help boost your visibility on the site, as well as key into your readers' specific interest. If they're searching for "Romance second chances," and they see it in your book description, it's going to ping them with: "Oh! This is exactly the book I've been looking for."

That said, avoid overstuffing your book description with keywords. I recommend using them if you can include them in an interview with the author or something similar (you can add this to your Amazon retail back via Author Central), but don't sacrifice a better description just to include more keywords. If you aren't familiar with Author Central, we'll discuss what it is an how to use it in a future chapter.

DON'T MARKET TO YOUR EGO

I often say to authors, "No one cares that you wrote a book." Family and friends may care, but they aren't your target audience. If you want to pull in readers—a lot of them—make sure your book appeals to *their* needs and *their* interests, not *yours*. If you're unsure about whether you've pulled this off, do a reader profile brainstorm or buyer market analysis to ensure you're aware of who your readers are and what makes them tick. You won't regret it because this knowledge is useful across the board in many facets of your promotion.

INCLUDE REVIEWS AND REWARDS

If you earned a standout review from a professional reviewer or book blogger, or if you won an award, highlight it in your description. Be smart about using the acclamation; and use excerpts instead of full quotes.

GET A SECOND OPINION

We're often too close to our own work to fully wrap our minds around what the market wants from us. From my own experience, I can tell you it's a delicate balance between teaching authors what I feel they need to learn and discussing problems they want me to address.

I'd strongly encourage you to get your editor's help when

writing your book's description or ask for feedback from other trusted individuals who know your market well, and take their suggestions and edits to heart.

UPDATE YOUR PAGE OFTEN

This is something you may not have considered: Your page isn't set in cement. In fact, ideally it shouldn't be static. When you receive positive reviews and awards, update your book page to reflect that. When you do your keyword string and category research every quarter (yes, put it on the list) consider whether there are any new ones you can sprinkle throughout the different sections on Author Central.

Here's another idea. If you're doing a special promotion, book promo, discount, or whatever, why not mention it in your book description?

I worked with a client this year who did a special bonus download on her website during the book's pre-order period, and I encouraged her to highlight it on her book description to drive even more engagements and downloads.

Finally, take a look at the book description below from Dan Silva. It's a good example of a blurb that combines great review quotes with a book description that pulls you in from the first sentence.

Book reviews are eye candy because people like what other people like. Even if you don't have review quotes from highly respected or recognizable publications such as *Booklist* and *Publishers Weekly*, you should still add reviews. Just be sure to cite them correctly.

Notice how they are boldfaced to draw attention? And check out the second paragraph. Whoever wrote this book description inserted a review to help bolster the character description, which is another clever idea.

The #1 *New York Times* Bestseller

"Fast-paced intrigue and provocative characters make this a fine addition to an outstanding series."—*People*, 4 stars

#1 *New York Times* bestselling author Daniel Silva delivers another stunning thriller in *The English Girl*—an action-packed tale of high stakes international intrigue starring art restorer and master spy Gabriel Allon.

When a beautiful young British woman vanishes on the island of Corsica, a prime minister's career is threatened with destruction. Gabriel Allon, the wayward son of Israeli intelligence, is thrust into a game of shadows where nothing is what it seems...and where the only thing more dangerous than his enemies might be the truth.

Silva's work has captured the imagination of millions worldwide; his #1 *New York Times* bestselling series which chronicles the adventures of art-restorer and master spy Gabriel Allon has earned the praise of readers and reviewers everywhere. This captivating page-turner from the undisputed master of spy fiction is sure to thrill new and old fans alike.

∧ Read less

Book descriptions are your sales pitch. The right description can help sell your book, so make sure yours is tightly written, exceptionally engaging, and aimed at turning a browser into a buyer.

WHY A GOOD ELEVATOR PITCH IS CRUCIAL TO YOUR SUCCESS (AND HOW TO CREATE ONE)

I f you've ever been pulled into a book by the enticing headline on the book retail page, chances are you were reading an elevator pitch.

At its core, an elevator pitch is a one- to two-sentence description that pulls the reader in via a story arc teaser or, in the case of nonfiction, the book's benefits. Elevator pitches (sometimes referred to as teasers) are impactful and always concise.

Elevator pitches, those enticing short bites that intrigue us and pull us into a movie, a product, or a book, are tremendously valuable to all of your marketing efforts. Sadly, most authors either don't do one or write a pitch that's too long and rambling to be interesting.

Why does this matter to your Amazon success? Remember when I talked about the Z-pattern readers use and how the eye scans your book page? Your elevator pitch, that first bit of content at the top of your book description, can make or break that initial scan for your potential reader.

You can also use your elevator pitch when you talk to bloggers, in all of your marketing materials, and as your Amazon ad copy. So if you're ready to rock your elevator pitch, let's dig in!

CHARACTERISTICS OF A STRONG ELEVATOR PITCH

First and foremost, your pitch needs to be concise. This means you say as much as possible using as few words as you can. As you write and review your pitch, cut out any unnecessary words. For example, many authors start their elevator pitches saying, "This book is about..." We know you're pitching a book; starting with "this book is about" is already making the mind wander.

Next, make sure it's compelling. Create a strong "why" or "wow, that's me" if you've written nonfiction or a memoir. The compelling element is core to your book, and though we're going to go into how to develop a solid elevator pitch in a minute, your elevator pitch should not include any extraneous details. Let's look at a few examples so you can see what I mean. I won't mention the book titles, just the blurbs so you can get a real sense of what you're trying to craft.

A simple yet revolutionary approach to improving your body's oxygen use, increasing your health, weight loss, and sports performance— whether you're a recovering couch potato or an Ironman triathlon champion. With a foreword by New York Times best-selling author Dr. Joseph Mercola.

This is one I found on the Amazon book page, and while it's okay, it's not great. First, I would drop the mention of the foreword.

Second, I'm not sure we care about oxygen use as much as what better breathing can do for us. And third, this book is trying to be too many things at once. The references to athletes (while I understand the connection) seem a bit out of left field. Let's look at what happens when we cut this down, leaving only the essential elements:

A better approach to weight loss and increasing your overall health may be as simple as better breathing.

Also, the prior version of this pitch sounded like a lot of work, and you really want to avoid that in any kind of book description, especially in your elevator pitch!

Now let's look at a fiction pitch:

Determined to become a police officer, 27-year-old Ally tries to hide a horrific secret about her sister's missing husband but as police uncover evidence about the missing man, she makes a mistake that threatens her life, the relationship with her sister, and any chance of wearing a badge.

This pitch is a bit long and confusing because the reader is drawn into too many conflicts. Including Ally's age in the first sentence isn't necessary. Why does her age matter? We aren't sure. But when you fill your elevator pitch with unnecessary details, the reader's mind pauses, trying to figure out what the book is about. The minute you pause readers' experience, you've lost them.

Determined to become a police officer, Ally tries to hide a horrific secret about her missing brother-in-law, but as police uncover new evidence on this unsolved case, she makes a mistake that threatens her life and any chance of ever wearing a badge.

I cut just enough to aid the flow and not distract the reader with details like the character's age. I removed one character. We already have the deceased brother-in-law, and too many additional people to track adds a layer to the elevator pitch that makes it feel sluggish.

Final point, and perhaps the most important one: your elevator pitch should clearly define your target market. When you share your pitch with agents, potential readers, etc., they should know immediately what genre your book is in. If they have to ask, you need to go back to the drawing board.

Let's break down the steps to create a powerful elevator pitch.

CREATING AN ELEVATOR PITCH IN THREE EASY STEPS

Step 1: What's your book about?

While this may sound easy, it really isn't. This is where authors often get lost. Why? Whether you've written fiction or nonfiction, we're always told to save the best for last. Make your reader get through most of the book before you turn the tables on your plot, or before two people (whom you know are destined to be together) finally see what the reader has seen all along. In nonfiction, we often save some of our best tips for last. The big statement or the big reveal is often found in the final chapters / pages of your book.

I'm not suggesting that you give away the "whodunit" or the secret sauce to the advice you're offering, but I do suggest that you have to dig deep to give readers the kind of "bite" from your story that will make them want to buy it.

The other element I want to mention is not using overly complex words when plain English will do. Save your five-dollar words for some other time and keep your pitches in very basic English.

Why? Because complex words don't sell books. I mentioned this in the last chapter, too. Writing book descriptions and elevator pitches (and media pitches) to an eighth-grade education level is easier on the brain and less likely to cause mental fatigue. Surprisingly, 73% of Americans read at a basic or intermediate level equivalent to an eighth-grade education. To put it another way, if you are writing any of your book marketing pieces—press release, book description, back cover copy—to a college-level reader, I can almost guarantee that you're missing out on sales.

The good news is that most word-processing programs come with a readability scoring system called Flesch-Kincaid. You can search for it in Word and it pops right up. Take a moment to find this and come back when you're ready. I'll be referring to this readability score often in this section, so you'll want to know where to find it.

Step 2: Give your pitch context

In the prior examples, I gave you a taste of what I mean by revealing enough of your book to whet their appetite, but not so much that you give away the entire story. Let's look at another example:

It's the story of how an Orange County housewife spent four years searching for her mother's murderer when law enforcement officials in both Mexico and the US gave up.

Remember how I discouraged you from saying "this book is about"? Well, starting a pitch with "it's the story of" makes the same mistake. It uses extraneous words. The other piece here that stops the readers' experience is the word "Mexico," which has no context in this pitch. Dropping the word "Mexico" from this pitch is step number one. Let's have a look at the pitch redone:

When law enforcement officials give up the search for her mother's murderer, an Orange County housewife spends 4 years searching both sides of the border for her mother's killer.

To refine this even more, you could say, "spends 4 years searching both sides of the border for the killer" instead of saying "her mother's killer." If we were pitching this to national media, I'd take out the words "Orange County" but put them back in if you're pitching local Orange County media. Why? Because that's context.

Step 3: Who Cares?

While it's not an easy question to ask yourself, it's an important one. In fact, it's a good question to ask yourself *anytime* you're writing anything related to your book, whether it's a press release, back-cover copy, or marketing copy. Who cares? We need to zero in on that before we send our marketing words out there in the world.

Let me give some context to the "who cares?" question. First, it's not about the importance of the work you're doing, but rather who will care about your book? One of the best ways to learn this craft is by digging through movie and TV loglines. These can easily be searched online, and it's a fun way to explore the "who cares?" question. Let's look at a few loglines I pulled up to give you some idea of what I'm talking about.

"An English combat nurse from 1945 is mysteriously swept back to 1743."

If you don't know the TV show or the book, this is the logline for *Outlander*. When you think about it, this logline makes a lot of sense for this audience, again answering that "who cares?" question. While the romance between the two lead characters is a driving force to the story, it's not mentioned at all in the logline. Why? The creator of this logline knows that readers (in this case, historical fiction readers) are focused less on the romance and more on the historical elements of the book/TV show. In fact, had the pitch mentioned the romance, it could have turned off a wide market for this book.

The essence of this example is this: know your readers.

In turn of the century London, a magical nanny employs music and adventure to help two neglected children become closer to their father.

This pitch is for *Mary Poppins*, and most of us are well aware of the storyline. But this logline creatively expresses a level of excitement. In twenty-three words, it weaves in magic, music, adventure, and a heartwarming element—all qualities associated with Disney.

This final logline is perhaps my favorite, not because of the movie (though it's a great one!) but of how superbly crafted the logline is.

After a single, career-minded woman is left on her own to give birth to the child of a married man, she finds a new romantic chance in a cab driver.

What's so amazing about this pitch is that nowhere is there a mention of the talking baby, which is a major part of the plotline. So why did the studio omit this from the logline? Why not say something like, "Bruce Willis creates the voice behind Mikey, this talking infant"? The marketers knew the majority of their moviegoers were probably moms, and the last thing they'd want to do is sit through 90 minutes of a kid talking. They could just stay home and listen to kids talking all day.

You can't create an elevator pitch in a vacuum. In fact, I encourage you to challenge yourself. Create three versions of your elevator pitch and share them on social; let your followers help you pick the right one, or give you some guidance on what they liked and didn't like. You could also share it with your newsletter readers, if you have a newsletter.

Elevator pitches are the core to a lot of what you'll do, whether it's pitching your book or creating a great ad for your Amazon ads. So take some time to create a few elevator pitches and then whittle them down as you go. Before you know it, you'll have a great elevator pitch that helps draw in more readers!

HOW TO WRITE A KICK-A** AMAZON BIO TO SELL MORE BOOKS

Authors often don't spend enough time crafting their bios. Most of them write up a quick "about me" to satisfy the basic requirements and never give it a second thought. I often see authors treat their bio like a resume. That approach is likely to bore readers. Worse, you risk making yourself look not only less interesting, but less interested in your own work and how you're coming across to readers.

Have I hit a nerve? Good!

Unless you tell me you know with certainty your bio is helping turn more browsers into buyers, I know for a fact I can help you make it better.

START WITH AN OUTLINE AND ALL BOOK TIE-INS

Before you begin, create a list or an outline of everything you've done related to the book. This can include life experiences, personal motivations, passion projects, research, past work in a related industry, accreditations, lectures and classes you've conducted, other books you've written, and awards you've won. You may ultimately include some of these elements, but not all of them. Listing all of these bullets will help you determine which to include.

BUT IT'S NOT REALLY ABOUT YOU

Although we start by focusing on you and your achievements, this bio actually isn't about you. It's about your readers and knowing what your prospective audience is looking for, what interests them, what catches their attention, and most importantly, what speaks to their needs.

Let's take a close look at a bio on Amazon by Mark Schaefer. His bio is keenly focused on his expertise as it relates to his book. Having read Mark's other books and having seen him speak, I can tell you he could have added a lot more to this, but he kept it short and relevant to the book.

Mark W. Schaefer

Mark W. Schaefer is a futurist and the bestselling author of some of the world's most beloved marketing books. He is the author of the world's first book on influencer marketing ("Return On Influence"), the bestselling book on Twitter ("Tao of Twitter), and seminal books like "The Content Code," "KNOWN" and "Marketing Rebellion" which are used as assigned texts in more than 50 universities.

His epic new book, "Belonging to the Brand: Why Community is the Last Great Marketing Strategy," is a spellbinding view of the massive potential of brand communities that can not only benefit businesses, but actually help heal the mental health challenges of our age. "Belonging to the Brand" soared to number one in the marketing category on Amazon, the sixth time Mark has achieved that status.

Mark's books weave significant research with gripping

storytelling, humor, and remarkable insights that place him among the most respected authors in the genre. His books have been translated into 20 languages and appear in more than 800 libraries.

The popularity of his books propelled Mark into a career as a captivating keynote speaker. He has spoken in more than 50 countries and on major stages such as SXSW (three keynotes), Social Media Marketing World (9X) and prestigious annual events like the American Bar Association, American Bankers Association, and the European Union's business think tank.

He is a globally-recognized educator, business consultant, and innovator (with seven patents). His well-known blog {grow} (www.businessesGROW.com), is one of the most acclaimed marketing blogs of the world and his Marketing Companion podcast, now in its tenth year, is in the top 1% of all business shows on iTunes.

He has advanced degrees in marketing and organizational development and has worked with AT&T, Microsoft, Pfizer, AllState Insurance, Adidas, and dozens of other global brands. He was the host and producer of Dell's first podcast. Mark is a faculty member of the graduate studies program at Rutgers University and has lectured at many universities including Oxford and Princeton. He has appeared as an expert marketing resource in the WSJ, New York Times, Wired, Forbes, Fortune, CBS News, and many other global media outlets.

WRITE IN THIRD PERSON

When it comes to writing a bio, never use words like "I" and "me." A bio written in the first person can make for an awkward read, especially when you're listing all your accomplishments. There are other options for getting personal. Don't worry!

SHOW THE READER YOUR EXPERTISE WITHOUT THE EGO

When it comes to the credible portion of the bio you are creating or reworking, this may seem tricky. But this is where the importance of your initial work comes in. How long have you been writing? Did you utilize any special techniques or resources in this book?

Check out Pete Ryan's bio. He's a first-time author, but he leads this bio with his background as a journalist, which tells the reader he is an experienced writer. Pete is also a marketing guy and has a successful business in SoCal. You'll notice he doesn't even mention it because it won't matter to his fiction readers, and Pete knows this.

Pete J. Ryan
Peter J. Ryan spent years as a journalist before venturing into the wilds of fiction writing. *Edge of the Sawtooth* is his first novel. A tireless backcountry hiker and overall outdoor enthusiast, Ryan splits his time between Huntington Beach, California and Paradise Valley, Montana. He is married with four grown children and three grandchildren.

ADD KEYWORD STRINGS PARTICULAR TO AMAZON

As I explained earlier, keyword strings matter greatly on Amazon. If you've already done your keyword string research, work some into your Amazon bio if you can keep it natural.

Don't cram your bio full of keywords just for the sake of having them there.

Why does this matter? Amazon is a search engine. Like a search engine, Amazon will "spider" or "crawl" your book page for keyword strings, so make sure at least one or two of the ones you've found are in your bio, but don't overdo it; readers will ding you for being inauthentic.

GET PERSONAL (IF APPROPRIATE)

There's a time and a place to include personal information in your bio. Obviously, it's essential to a memoir. For a self-help book, your connection to the topic is crucial. But if you're a novelist, you can also get personal in a creative way because your personality says a lot about your brand.

The key is finding the right balance. For example, if you write paranormal fantasy, the fact that you coach your daughter's softball team may sound endearing, but it doesn't fit your genre. On the other hand, if you've always had a fascination with mythology and history, and it fuels your stories, that's great insight into who you are.

BE FUNNY (IF APPROPRIATE)

Be like what you wrote about. If your book is funny, be funny. Check out this bio from Karen Alpert. Her book is *I Heart My Little A-Holes: A bunch of holy-crap moments no one ever told you about parenting.*

+ Follow

Follow to get new release updates, special offers (including promotional offers), and improved recommendations.

About Karen Alpert

Karen is the ridiculously hairy, self-deprecating writer of the popular blog Baby Sideburns. You may have seen a few of her more viral posts like "What NOT to F'ing buy my kids this holiday" and "Caillou sucks so bad, here's another blog about why I hate him." She spent fifteen years working for national advertising agencies until she was promoted to her newest favorite job— Mommy. She lives with her two amazing kiddos and a very forgiving husband who is kind enough not to call her Cousin It when she undresses for bed every night.
⌃ Read less

SHORT IS THE NEW LONG

The days of bios that rival the length of your book are gone. Keep it short because, while people do care who wrote the book, they don't care enough to read paragraphs upon paragraphs about you. Save the long bio for your website, the foundation of your infrastructure, and where readers will go when they want to learn even more about you!

INCLUDE A CALL TO ACTION AND TELL READERS HOW TO FIND YOU

Do you want your readers to take any action besides buying your book? Are you giving something away on your website? Do you want readers to join your exclusive reader group or your newsletter? Then mention these offers in your bio. Don't forget to add your website address so they can find you.

CUSTOMIZE IT AND CHANGE IT UP

Your life isn't static, and your bio shouldn't be either. Is there something going on in the world that ties into your book? Mention it! You should also modify your bio when you win awards, get more mentions, or get some fab new reviews. For example, *"The New York Times* calls this book 'groundbreaking'" is a review quote you could easily add at the end of your bio for a strong finish. An upcoming release or mention of your other work is another reason to tweak your bio.

Find reasons to change your bio. You can do it as often as you want, and the algorithms notice and respond when a book page is updated.

If you're with a traditional publisher, you may be thinking, "The publisher won't let me change my bio!" Trust me, you don't need your publisher to make changes. Just do it on your Amazon Author Central dashboard and—voilà—done and done.

Your bio should be a fluid extension of your author brand, so update it as part of your monthly book marketing plan. This may seem tedious, but it serves another purpose: it gets your eyes on your entire book page, and once you're there, hopefully you will be inspired to cast a critical eye on other parts of the page and make updates that could help drive more sales.

AMAZON EBOOK PRICING TIPS

Book pricing is another way you can activate the Amazon system to boost your ranking.

It's important to understand the Amazon royalty system. When you publish through KDP, you can choose either a 35% or a 70% royalty. Initially you might say 70% is a no-brainer. But there's more involved in the decision than you might think.

Amazon has a "sweet spot" when it comes to pricing. The highest-rated eBooks are generally priced between $2.99 and $9.99, with the ideal price for some genres (particularly genre fiction) around $5.99. That doesn't mean you won't see higher-priced books in top categories, but they typically will bounce up for a brief period and then vanish. Consistent sales require better, smarter pricing, especially for first-time authors.

Many authors price their books based on word count. While there's some merit to this approach, keep in mind that if you price your eBook over $10, you could be pricing yourself out of the market, especially if you're a first-time author. Remember, you're asking readers to take a chance on you and your book. This is one reason it's important not to overprice your book.

There's another element to eBook pricing, and that's changing the price point of your book on a semiregular basis. You could have a $1.99 sale, or you could have a free eBook promotion. You could also drop the price of the book for a week during launch time to help boost your algorithm results.

My point is your price doesn't have to remain static. You could reduce it when you run specials, promote new books, or have another reason. This doesn't mean you should change the price of your book daily, or even weekly. But if you have more than one book, you could certainly have at least one of them on sale all the time.

Generally, if an author has three or more titles, I recommend they rotate them in terms of pricing to help their Amazon algorithm. If you have just one book, changing the price of it once a month winds up training your potential buyers to simply wait for the lower price. So be mindful of this if you have just one book. However, keeping your books at the same price is never a good idea if you want to attract more readers.

PART THREE
SUCCESSFUL BOOK LAUNCHES ON AMAZON

YOUR FIRST 30 DAYS ON AMAZON

ere's the scenario: you work incredibly hard to finish your book, you upload it to Amazon or send it to your publisher and—voilà!—your work is done. Now you can sit back and enjoy the moment, right?

Wrong.

This kind of scenario won't benefit you, and it certainly won't benefit your book. But this is what most authors do. It's not because an author is lazy. In most cases, it's a matter of not being sure what to do next, where to start, or how to launch a book correctly.

The issue with working this way is that while you're trying to figure out how to promote your book or waiting for that review to appear on Amazon, your book starts to "sink" down the rankings on Amazon. This is problematic because when a book sinks too far and too fast down the Amazon system, it won't stay on the "new release" list very long (and I'll talk a bit later about why this is important). But it also doesn't "trigger" Amazon to do anything with the book. The Amazon algorithm knows that anyone can publish a book, and the algorithm also knows that not everyone markets the book right out of the gate. Authors who don't market their books early tend not to market them at all. That's been my experience anyway, and I believe the Amazon algorithm is built with much the same understanding.

The issue here again is not so much that authors are lazy but that book launches are largely misunderstood.

Most of the time, when we think about book launches, we think about a first week filled with media appearances and blogger reviews. We envision the first book signing on the day the book is "born" on Amazon with a line of fans around the corner. For some authors, this happens, but for most of us, this isn't reality. Authors often focus on what is perceived as a "traditional" launch when, in reality, there is no such thing. And while you're focused on what a traditional launch should feel like, your book starts to sink down the Amazon bestseller list until it's near the bottom and almost impossible to find in a search.

When you first load your book onto Amazon (or your publisher does), Amazon's algorithms work hard to try and "learn" your book. By "learn," I mean the site wants to know a few things:

- What genre is this book in?
- Will readers like this book?
- Will we want to push it to consumers?

Almost all of these questions are answered in the first 30 days of the life of your book. I am focusing on book launches on Amazon because most of them aren't done correctly.

Let's consider Google for a moment. In prior chapters, I've discussed how the Google algorithm is similar to Amazon's. For example, let's say you launch your website with no keywords, no alt tags (picture titles), no blog. It's just a site with your picture, your bio, and maybe your book cover. Google will look at this site and shrug its virtual shoulders, not knowing where to categorize your website. Soon, your site will be relegated to page 54 of the Google search platform, never to be found again. Yes, you can add keywords and optimize it later, but it will still be a struggle to get found. The same principle applies to Amazon.

At my firm, we have a pre-order campaign, which focuses on a short pre-order window to help boost the book and trigger the algorithms. To some degree, this helps to force the Amazon system to "learn" where this book belongs and categorize it correctly. This can also help you stay on the "new releases" list, which is a fun and potentially lucrative place to be.

In the next few chapters, I'm going to unpack our methodology for this approach, along with some tips and tricks and insider scoop so you can do this on your own.

HOW TO BOOST YOUR ORGANIC OPTIMIZATION WITH AMAZON'S PRE-ORDER

One of the newer features on Amazon that I am most excited to discuss in the revised edition of this book is the algorithm boost you get from a well-executed pre-order campaign. As many of you probably already know, Amazon allows eBook pre-orders for KDP authors, which essentially levels the playing field between traditionally published authors and those who self-publish through KDP. (Note: Amazon will be expanding this pre-order option to paperback books in 2024, so be on the lookout!)

If you're working with a publishing house, indie publisher, or hybrid publisher, the publisher will likely set this up for you, though the rules still apply.

I'll take you through the steps to get your book into pre-order, but first let's look at when and how this strategy may benefit you.

Amazon's Kindle Pre-Order information page says pre-orders are great for building buzz. True.

But there is a caveat. If you're a new author who hasn't built a reader base, you really have to power through your pre-order and work harder than if you had a series of books already published. In the past, most authors used pre-orders to boost sales to hit a bestseller list right out of the gate; while for some that's certainly a consideration, the majority of authors should consider other goals.

Sure, bestseller status would be great, but an organic algorithm boost right out of the gate—which benefits you long-term—would be even better.

THE NEWLY PUBLISHED AUTHOR

If you're a newly published author, the idea of a pre-order is probably very appealing. Your book is up on the Amazon site while you count down the days to its release.

It *is* pretty exciting, but spend your marketing time wisely. Don't spend a ton of time marketing your pre-order page at this point because even if you have a fan base you likely won't get a ton of orders. You can do a small push to friends and family and to a mailing list if you have one, but at this point it's smarter to start playing with Amazon ads, categories, and keyword strings to help the Amazon algorithm kick in.

Your work should be divided into the pieces that help kick-start the algorithm on Amazon (which will benefit you long-term) and the work you can do after the book launches. We'll look at a specific pre-order plan later on in the book.

YOU'RE ALREADY PUBLISHED

If you already have published one or more books and you've built a mailing list of fans, pre-order can build excitement for your new book. But most, if not all, of your marketing should be reserved for when the book is available on Amazon because that will result in a much bigger benefit for you.

Unless you are J.K. Rowling or some other mega-bestselling author, it's not easy to drive significant numbers to your pre-order page. Another obstacle is that people are impatient so if they want to read something now, they may not want to wait for your book to be available; they could end up buying something else instead.

That said, pre-order can be a lot of fun for fans who've been waiting for your next book.

But even if you're an established author, your pre-order efforts should be focused on giving an algorithm kick to your Amazon book page, which is the smart long-term approach.

LONG VS. SHORT PRE-ORDERS

Regardless of your book's category, don't stretch the pre-order time to the full 90 days Amazon allows. And if you have a publisher who wants to do a yearlong pre-order, ask why. Some publishers are tethered to distribution contracts that require long pre-orders. If the publisher says, "Well, it's what we've done before" ask whether the company would reconsider this long of a pre-order period and explain your reasons. Once you've finished this section, you'll have all the answers to that!

So how long should your pre-order period be? I'd recommend a month or less; my ideal actually would be two weeks. But those two weeks should be spent on a solid, focused effort which we'll walk through shortly.

Why do I recommend such a brief period? Most consumers don't want to wait for a book. We live in an impatient society. If you're doing a lot of promotion and directing lots of eyes to a pre-order for a book that isn't launching for a few months (or longer), don't be surprised if your pre-order sales are lower than you had hoped. Someone may see your ad, or whatever pre-order promotion you have going, and think, "That's a good idea, but I need a book now so I'll get this other one." However, most people are willing to wait two weeks to get a book they *really* want.

THE AMAZON ALGORITHM FOR PRE-ORDERS

As I said earlier in this book, when it comes to Amazon, everything matters. This includes your pre-order.

I discovered this with the last edition of this book, which I put up for pre-order for two weeks. I started pushing Amazon ads as soon as the book page went live, and the early ad run helped boost the book up the bestseller list. We also did a promotion, which we'll talk about in the next section.

The bottom line: there's a certain amount of momentum that a book captures organically when it launches on Amazon. It sits in the "new release" section of Amazon, which can be a great spot to attract additional interest.

However, if your book is on pre-order and then hits the Amazon system on launch day with little to no buzz, no reviews, and no activity, it'll quickly plummet due to low sales, which is really hard to recover from.

Books that sink down the Amazon list on launch day can take a long time to resurrect. In the testing I've done, the recovery sometimes takes three months or longer. Even if you have no immediate reviews, ads will help keep the book spiking within its category.

To avoid your book dropping precipitously on Amazon, you need to plan a solid promotional campaign for the day it launches..

PRE-ORDER PROMOTION STRATEGIES

You can start to drive some interest to the book by letting your followers know it's coming. However, be warned that your relationship with your followers needs to be about more than just pushing your book. That will get old fast and could lose you buyers. In my book *From Book to Bestseller*, I discuss how to use newsletters, how to warm up your list, and how to market consistently without publishing the sales message.

You can also use your cover or other images in social media posts, blog posts, Amazon ads, and so on to promote your book.

Promotions and giveaways are other ways to build interest during the pre-order period. When a prior edition of this book launched, we decided to do a new kind of promotion. It was essentially a buy one, get one—but instead of gifting a second book, we gave readers who pre-ordered the Amazon book access to our Master Amazon Video Program.

It went so well that we repeated it for the 2022 edition. The push for pre-orders within a short window helped the book build up a strong head of steam before the actual launch day, when it just exploded. In fact, if you've taken one of my classes recently, you know I lead off discussing all the bestseller status ribbons this book has earned.

Sometimes these flags last days or months, other times they last just hours. But regardless of how long you get a bestseller flag, if you've ever had one, you know how incredible it feels, right?

In previous editions of the book, we've given away second copies of the book so a customer can buy one and gift one to a friend. That's been popular and is certainly a sound strategy, but if you have anything else to give readers access to, that might generate an even stronger motivation for them to pre-order. You could give them one of your other books for free if they buy your current one; if the book is part of a series, you could gift them an earlier book in the series. Some authors give tote bags. Make the "gift" as creative and original as you can.

Whether this is your first or tenth book, to promote your pre-order properly, you'll need to do more than just buzz it to your followers and your email list. Again, if this is your second, third, or fourth book, interest is going to be stronger than with your first.

But offering some kind of a promotional bonus will always help boost sales!

GETTING REVIEWS

Keep in mind that readers can't review a book on pre-order. If you're looking to get some early reviews, consider focusing on Goodreads, where you can push for pre-order reviews and provide advance reader copies (ARCs) to potential reviewers. You could also do an early giveaway. If you aren't familiar with Goodreads, I wrote a whole chapter on that as well as doing a giveaway in my book: From Book to Bestseller!

PRICING YOUR PRE-ORDER

As mentioned earlier, there's a sweet spot in pricing. Keep the price low(ish), even if you plan to raise it later. You're competing with millions of titles on Amazon, and your book hasn't even been released. If you want to entice an impulse buy, keep the pricing slightly lower at first. Once the book is live, you can always raise the price, or you can wait through a certain window. You might keep the introductory price lower for 30 days or so, then raise it after that.

HOW TO SET UP YOUR PRE-ORDER ON THE KDP DASHBOARD

First and foremost, you need to be a KDP author. Your eBook should be uploaded into the KDP system via the author/book dashboard. Once you're there, you'll see this:

Once you select a date, the system will tell you that you must get the final book to Amazon no later than four days before that date. Additionally, you will need to upload a manuscript before you can set up your pre-order. The manuscript doesn't have to be pre-edited; Amazon just wants to see what you plan to publish. You'll need a cover, but it doesn't have to be a final version. If you're still a month out with no cover (it happens more often than you think), you can leave the cover blank or put up a placeholder, then add your cover before the pre-order goes live.

According to Amazon, the book can be any length, so you can use pre-order if you've written a novella, too. Currently there are no limitations, other than that you need to be a KDP author, *and if you're an indie author, this is for eBooks only.*

Pre-order is a fun option for self-published authors, but be mindful of how much money and promotional sweat equity you spend. Most readers prefer to buy a book they can read right away. The urge for instant gratification is especially true for eBook readers, because for them, it truly is instant.

THE PERIL OF AMAZON'S ALSO-BOUGHTS

Book marketing is tough enough without having to wrestle your Amazon book page into submission, too. With Amazon book pages getting increasingly cluttered, it's become harder to find your book among the clutter of ads, sidebar stuff, and everything else Amazon is pushing.

If you read the Author Marketing Experts blog regularly, you probably know what a book marketing pet peeve this is for me. In fact, I'm kind of a fanatic about keeping that book page clean and user-friendly. This "look" includes your also-boughts—that ribbon of books sandwiched somewhere between your book description, the sponsored posts, and whatever else Amazon is trying to sell to your reader.

Also-bought lists are populated by consumers who visit your book page. Let's take a reader who normally buys romantic suspense books, lands on your book, reads the description, maybe reads a few reviews, but then realizes this isn't the book for him or her. It happens, right? Let's say the reader in question normally buys books on car mechanics or poetry or something completely different from what you've written.

Guess what happens? It changes your also-boughts. This algorithm is based on simply landing on your page. I've tested this with my own books, inviting folks who don't normally buy books on book marketing to just land on the page without making a purchase. Guess what happened? My also-boughts changed!

It happens frequently. Authors publish a book and excitedly email all their friends to buy a copy. Some will, and some won't, but it's likely that they will visit the book page, even out of curiosity. Now, if all of your friends buy books in your genre, you're fine, but if Aunt Bethany normally buys books on quilting and you've just published your new sci-fi thriller—guess what? Quilting books will start to populate in your also-bought section.

Why does this matter? Because when it comes to Amazon, everything matters.

E-V-E-R-Y-T-H-I-N-G matters.

Don't ignore your also-boughts! Let's have a look at some reasons, both organic and visual, why this feature matters to your book sales.

WHY ALSO-BOUGHTS MESS WITH YOUR ALGORITHM

It's hard to prove the Amazon algorithm; it's an invisible force at work behind the scenes, so it's increasingly challenging to figure out what tips it in your favor and what does not. What I know from books I've tested is that having a messed-up list of also-boughts does impact your visibility on Amazon. It makes sense, right? There isn't an actual person shelving the also-boughts on your page; it's a machine—and machine learning can be tricky.

Machines learn what you show them, and if you show that quilting books belong with sci-fi, that's how your book will start showing up, and that's where Amazon will think your book belongs. See the problem? This could impact everything you're doing on Amazon, from running Amazon ads to having discounted eBook promotions—everything. In a minute, I'll cover what to do and how to fix this problem if it's happening to you.

MAY MISRANK YOUR BOOK(S)

Much as they can mess with your algorithm, the also-boughts can also misrank your books. You will notice this when you look at the book details and see your book listed in some odd category. Book details are located in the middle of your book page. Included in the book details are things like page count and year of publication. Misranking is a problem for your Amazon relevancy score, too. So if your time management book is ranking lower than thrillers or romance, it can impact your relevancy score.

INTERRUPT THE USER EXPERIENCE

When I teach classes on website SEO, ranking, and how to attract people to your website, I talk about the user experience. You want to keep everything on your website in line with user expectations. This means if you're selling books about car mechanics, don't include a picture of your new puppy. That's not why people landed on your website.

The same is true for your Amazon book page. As I mentioned earlier, I'm a fanatic about a good user experience, and part of that is your also-boughts. Interrupting the user experience by showing quilting books on your sci-fi book page could lead to losing browsers—because it takes less than a second to lose a browser on your site. This may not seem like a concern to you, but in the world of web design and user experience, it's huge. Your Amazon book page is an extension of your website and, as I mentioned before, everything matters.

PREVENTING AN ALSO-BOUGHT MIX-UP

This part is both easy and difficult. The first days your book is live on Amazon are the most critical. Because Amazon is still "learning" about your book, you have no history with Amazon for that particular title, and machine learning is busy trying to understand your title.

As hard as it may seem, I encourage you not to invite all your family and friends to your book page, at least not right away. Wait till the also-boughts have started populating, which could take a few weeks. I know it's hard. You just published a book, and you want to share it with the world. I get it. But trust me, it's more difficult to clean up a potential mess later.

Alternatively, if your family and friends are a bit internet-savvy, you could invite them to visit your book from an incognito page, which won't pull in any potential buyer preferences, although they won't be able to buy your book that way.

A better option would be to invite them to your website, where you can sell your book *and* autograph it for them. Yes, you'll have to mail the books—but you'll also get to personalize them. People (especially friends and family) will love this special touch, and if your launch is around a holiday period (and even if it's not) offer a BOGO: if someone buys your book from your website, offer to send an eBook to a friend of that buyer.

RESOLVING MESSED-UP ALSO-BOUGHTS

If you're saying, "Yes, I have a bunch of quilting books on my sci-fi book page," you're probably wondering whether there's anything you can do about it.

Two things: First, you can start to promote the heck out of your book to the right market. But be aware that, in some cases, it can take 90 days for also-boughts to fix themselves.

Second, a messed-up list of also-boughts doesn't last forever. It will eventually right itself, but it will take time. Running Amazon ads could speed up the process because if your keywords are exactly the right ones, you're pulling exactly the right readers to your book.

When it comes to Amazon, keeping an eye on that ever-important book page is a critical component of your success. Whether it's the also-boughts, your book description, or the million other fun things you can do with that page—remember, it all matters.

Final note: As of this writing the also-boughts were still a "thing" on Amazon, though there's a chance that Amazon may get rid of these, in favor of more book ads so we'll see. Everything is change on Amazon all the time, so it's worth mentioning that there may come a time when Amazon gets rid of these altogether.

PART FOUR
ROCKETING YOUR BOOK TO SUCCESS WITH AMAZON ADVERTISING

THE SURPRISING BENEFITS OF RUNNING AMAZON ADS

n this chapter we're going to learn all about Amazon ads. But before we do that, we need to set the stage, so ask yourself: Why am I running Amazon ads?

First and foremost, I love Amazon ads because, unlike Facebook ads, someone landing on Amazon is more than likely ready to buy. And while some authors do very well with Facebook ads, consider this: you still need to get viewers to click over to your Amazon retail page, and every time you ask a consumer to click online, you lose 20% of your audience. So Amazon ads are a direct link to your buyer, without question.

Why run Amazon ads? It's not an unreasonable question. Some authors run ads because they feel they have to while others run them because someone in their writing group is running them and doing really well.

You need to figure out your "why," or you won't know if your ads are meeting your goals. If you're unfamiliar with ads in general, determining your goals may seem impossible. Even if you know your goals, I suspect you'll change your mind after you read this chapter. So whatever preconceived ideas you have around running ads, let's put them aside for a minute and unwrap some of the surprising benefits Amazon ads offer you.

When Amazon launched its ads about four years ago, many authors jumped on the Amazon ad-system bandwagon. The ads seemed simple enough, and the results seemed darned good.

Soon enough, however, Amazon realized it was onto something even more profitable than the ad revenue, and Amazon Marketing Services (AMS) was born. Now, in 2023, Amazon is actively looking to compete with Google in terms of ad systems—and, as you'll see from this chapter, it's getting very close to it.

THE BIGGEST BENEFIT OF AMAZON ADS

The biggest benefit of the ads system is exposure. And I'm not just talking about the ability to get a consumer to click through to your page. I'm talking about the fact that within the Amazon ads system, you don't pay for Amazon to show your ad; you only pay when a potential reader clicks on the ad.

So, why does this matter? Exposure sells books and the more you can get your book cover in front of your potential buyer, the more likely you are to sell books. The marketing rule of seven comes into play here. That rule says it takes a consumer seven impressions of your book or message before they take action. Yes, sometimes consumers take action right away but in most cases, consumers really need to see your message multiple times before they'll take action. This is why the Amazon ads are so valuable. You absolutely want potential readers to click your ad; if they don't and only "see" your cover, you may feel as if you lost a sale. In reality, you're starting to build awareness.

For this reason, I want to caution you about taking Amazon's sales dashboard (on its AMS site) too literally. We'll discuss this more in the section titled: Understanding Amazon Ad Metrics, but the sales reporting on the ads leaves a lot to be desired.

Let's say you've been running ads for your book for a while with lackluster sales from your ads. While it could be that your ads just aren't working, you may have the wrong set of keywords or maybe your cover isn't the best. But what if you're running ads and though the ads aren't showing many sales, your book has definitely picked up steam when it comes to selling copies? Check out your sales dashboard before killing off your ads. Take note of your book sales and/or page reads (if you're in Kindle Unlimited) before you started running ads, and keep tabs on these numbers as your ads start to gain in visibility. The reason to do this is that some ads may not get clicks but still raise exposure for your book. And the first time the consumer sees your ad, he or she may think the book looks interesting. After repeated exposure, the person decides to head over to your book page (sometimes without clicking the ad itself) and, boom, you've made a sale.

Yes, we want our ads to result in clicks and sales, but losing sight of one of the biggest benefits the ads offer means you'll miss one of the strongest incentives to run ads. But wait, there's more. Let's dig into more benefits and unpack the secrets behind the Amazon algorithm.

More Benefits to Amazon Ads!

The other big benefit? Unlike advertising on Facebook, Instagram, or Google, people who land on the Amazon site are literally there to buy. Consider this: the average conversion rate for a Google ad is 3.75%, whereas the average conversion rate for Amazon is 10%.

UNPACKING THE ADS ALGORITHM

Unlike Google, the Amazon platform derives some *organic* optimization from your ads, which means your ads can help with visibility. Seems pretty obvious, right? But it can also help you in other ways. Let me explain.

I was trying to find more keywords to aid my book's visibility and my rank—and add to my ads. I hadn't added "marketing on Amazon" yet, so I decided to start by including it in my ad set, even before adding it to the book page itself. Before I added it to my book description, or to my keywords dashboard, I discovered that adding it to my ad set helped it show up *organically* under that search string. So even before the keyword was cycled into the ad set (which takes 24 to 48 hours), my book was already showing up under this search.

Keywords that you add to your ads help your rank, not just for the ads, but for the keywords, which is why I love doing keyword-based ads. In part 5, we're going to talk more about keyword-based ads and product-based ads. Normally I wouldn't suggest running one without the other, and I certainly wouldn't run a product-based ad without a keywords ad, because it's the keywords that will help you optimize your book in ways that you *technically* don't have to pay for.

KICK-STARTING THE ORGANIC RECOMMENDATION ENGINE

Ads do more than promote your book. Ads are a way to kick-start organic growth for your book. They push your book onto the radar screen of readers, yes, but they're also a way to drive more organic sales to your book page, and not just from the ads. Let me explain.

When I was playing around with ads for the 2020 edition of this book, I decided to run an ad set ahead of the launch, so I ran it during the pre-order, which I had set up for two weeks. During that time, we were also pushing the special I mentioned in the pre-order section of this book. But I also ran ads, and I copied an existing ad set for the prior edition of *The Amazon Author Formula* (previously called *How to Sell Books by the Truckload on Amazon*), added some more words, and let it run during the pre-order time, a full two weeks.

This, combined with the offer, helped to push the book into bestseller status and kick-started the organic recommendation engine.

This boost allowed the book to sit in bestseller status for months; in fact, even as I write, it's rocketing back up the bestseller list again. Once that organic recommendation engine kicks in, and you have all of the other pieces in place—good book, good cover, great book description, and so on—it can help your book in ways you can't even imagine.

Let me add that I'm not spending a ton on ads. The ad set I ran during launch cost me about $50 for three weeks. Now it's around $120 a month, and I sell five or six times that in books each month. Worth it, right?

DO ADS NEED TO BE PROFITABLE?

This may seem like an odd question. Obviously, you want to sell books, but in some cases, it's a fine line. Maybe you only care about the optimization that the ads will bring to your book page, in which case you may only care about breaking even. The other reason for this is because Amazon tracks ad sales, but as I mentioned earlier, the ads dashboard doesn't track all sales. Keeping an eye on your overall book sales will tell you if your ads are really operating at break-even or at a loss. In many cases, I've seen ads that are doing okay, but the algorithm has kicked in so that the book is selling even if the ads aren't showing a high-profit outcome.

THE RELEVANCY OF YOUR AMAZON ADS

I've talked about the "relevancy score" that Amazon gives all ads, and while it's hard to figure out how that ranking actually works, it has a lot to do with impressions and click-through rates.

Relevancy goes beyond that. What Amazon means here is the

relevance of the book related to the search string or product. It's often tempting to anchor your book to the overall Amazon best-seller list and start populating your ads with these mega-best-sellers, but that lowers the overall relevancy score of your ad set, which means it will get harder to show your ads, if not impossible. Your ads will also start costing more. **When I evaluate author ads campaigns, this is the number one issue I see.**

Be careful to choose books and keywords (and authors) that are closely related to what your book is about. While it may seem like a great idea to ride the coattails of famous authors, the reader won't see it that way. A bad ad set can hurt your overall account because the relevancy score will impact other ads. I've mentioned this several times in this section because it is so important.

PART FIVE
AMAZON ADS—THE BASICS

GETTING STARTED WITH AMAZON ADS

f this is your first time researching Amazon ads, start here. We'll briefly walk you through the ads options and setup. But if this isn't your first rodeo and you have ads running but are ready to learn more about optimizing them for better visibility and a lower cost, skip to the next chapter.

So let's dig into how to set up your first set of ads!

- Sign up for an Amazon advertising account. If you don't have an Amazon advertising account, create one by going to https://advertising.amazon.com/ and clicking on "Sign In" in the top right-hand corner. Follow the prompts to create your account.
- If you aren't a KDP author, you'll need to access your Amazon ads via your Author Central account: author.amazon.com. From there click on the Marketing tab and log in.
- Choose your campaign type: Amazon offers several types of campaigns, including Sponsored Products, Sponsored Brands, Sponsored Display, and Sponsored Video (not widely available yet). Choose the campaign

type that best suits your advertising goals. If you're not certain, hang tight. We'll discuss more about each of these types of ads in future chapters.

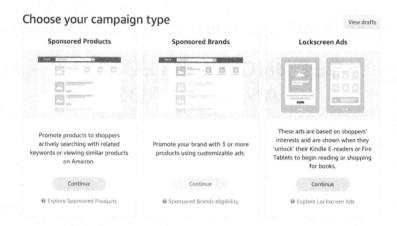

- Choose your ad type: either Custom Text Ad or Standard Text Ad. (We'll discuss both later on in this section).

- Select your book from the list of books under your name. Hint: If you don't see yours there, you may have to add it via Author Central.
- Select your targeting options. Pick either automatic or manual. If you select manual targeting, the page will change to give you the option to do keyword targeting or product targeting.
- Depending on what you select, the next Amazon

dropdown will change, allowing you to enter either products or keywords.

- Set your budget. Determine your budget for your campaign and set a daily budget accordingly.
- Name your campaign: if you're running multiple campaigns, give them descriptive names. It'll be easier to monitor campaigns if you use names.
- Create your ad. Use Amazon's ad builder to create your ad. This process will vary depending on the campaign type you selected. Follow Amazon's ad guidelines, and ensure that your ad is compelling and relevant to your target audience.
- Launch your campaign: Once you have set up your campaign, reviewed it for accuracy, and made any necessary changes, you can launch your campaign. You'll get an email from Amazon stating that the ads campaign is pending approval. Once Amazon has approved it, you'll get another email saying that the campaign has launched.

UNDERSTANDING DIFFERENT TYPES OF AMAZON ADS

As we explore Amazon ads, we're going to look at several different ad types: Sponsored product ads—automatic, keyword and product placements, and brand ads. Amazon Ads continue to evolve, so let's unpack each of the options available to you.

WHAT KIND OF ADS CAN YOU CREATE?

As of this writing, the video ads have not launched to a broader audience, so we're going to focus on the various ad type Amazon currently offers:

1. Sponsored product ads (automatic, keyword or product focused)
2. Lock-screen ads
3. Brand ads
4. Video ads (though not offered to everyone as of this writing)

Sponsored product ads can appear in a variety of ways,

depending on whether you're using keywords, categories, or actual products, so we'll discuss the pros and cons of each option. Brand ads appear at the top of the search page and tend to be more expensive because the top of the search page is the coveted Amazon space.

Amazon lock-screen ads currently show up only on Kindle devices, meaning your ad won't appear unless your reader has an actual Kindle device, not the Kindle app. Kindle device reader demographics may determine whether you opt to do these ads. For example, fiction readers tend to read on actual Kindles, not the Kindle app on a laptop, iPhone, iPad, or other tablet.

For the purposes of this section, I'm going to focus on sponsored product ads, for both keywords and products; brand ads; and automatic ads, since my testing of the lock-screen ads wasn't favorable. I found it difficult to get books approved into this particular ad segment, and once I did, the return on investment (ROI) just wasn't there.

PRODUCT TARGETING

Although product targeting ads take a bit more time to set up, they pair well with almost any book genre. And since you can pull in a specific product, the targeting can be much more precise.

Product targeting works exactly as the name implies. You're tethering your ad to a specific book either through the ISBN or Amazon's ASIN number assigned to eBooks published on the site directly.

Within product targeting, you can also target categories, which is great up to a point because Amazon constantly changes how categories are shown to the reader. Therefore, it's doubtful that you'll get as many clicks from your category ads as you do from the ISBNs, ASINs, or book titles you've assigned with it but it's still worth doing. Why? As you'll see when we dig into the metrics of Amazon ads, it's all about building pathways.

The only drawback to these ads is the cost. Product targeting ads tend to cost a bit more to run because of the precise targeting you can do, aligning your ad with the exact right book and book format.

Keep in mind that product targeting ads don't show up in search results but rather on the "products related to this item" carousel, like this:

Amazon is always testing this, too. Most recently I've seen a carousel with sponsored product ads that had four-star and higher reviews only. And Amazon indicated this at the top: "4-Star and Above Only," it read. This means that if your book doesn't hit that star rating, your ad won't show in that carousel. Whether Amazon is beta-testing this or not, I can't be sure, but it's worth mentioning and keeping an eye on as Amazon is always making changes.

KEYWORD TARGETING

The term "keyword targeting" is a misnomer. As we talked about earlier in this book, the term "keyword" actually means a keyword string or keyword phrase. If you're running ads with just single keywords (e.g., mystery, romance, or self-help), you're probably spending a lot of money on ads without generating many sales.

I prefer keyword targeting for almost every campaign I manage because it allows me to get specific in terms of where a book is placed.

The only issue with keyword targeting is that you don't control where Amazon shows your book in terms of what book *format* it aligns your ad with. We know some consumers prefer eBooks over print, or audiobooks over print and eBook. However, with keyword targeting, Amazon can place your ads by any format of book. Is this problematic? Not if all of your book formats are connected on Amazon (and I've seen lots of authors forget to do this, believe it or not). The other issue is the speed at which consumers decide to buy a book. For example, let's say Amazon shows your eBook in a list of print titles in a market where print is preferred. You may get a consumer who says, "Oh, I don't read eBooks" and then skips your ad altogether without clicking the book link. It's a small thing but worth mentioning because reader preferences are important. And we'll dig more into that in a bit.

One cautionary statement on keyword targeting: be careful of book titles as keywords. Though I like using the title in keyword strings, if there are multiple books with the same title, your ad could get presented to the wrong audience.

AUTOMATIC TARGETING

Although it seems like the easiest option, automatic targeting has some pitfalls. First, automatic targeting relies on your book's algorithm, which means your book title, keywords, and categories. It also relies (to a certain extent) on your also-boughts.

Some authors will tell you that automatic ads are highly effective, and they certainly can be. But they can also be expensive because you're essentially telling Amazon to run your campaign for you and, even though Amazon doesn't drive through budgets the way Google AdWords or Facebook does, you can still spend a whole lot of money on a whole lot of nothing.

For this reason, it's often tricky for authors to run automatic ads for newly released books, especially if it's a first book and it's not been properly optimized.

Automatic targeting is really just the Amazon algorithm taking over, and if you've done nothing to optimize your book, your ads may end up being a bit of a free-for-all.

One way to narrow the targets for these ads is by using search terms, which we'll discuss in a minute.

Before we examine ads further, let's first explain some Amazon ad standards and best practices. First, let's discuss the all-important buying habits of your reader.

BRAND ADS

The beauty of these ads is that they're shown at the top of a search results page on Amazon, which is every author's dream. Positioning your book at the top of some of the most valuable real estate is powerful, which is one reason I love brand ads on Amazon.

Brand ads do, however, require that you have a minimum of three books, though they don't have to be in a series. I've run brand ads for my titles on book marketing that are not in a series. They just have to be three unique titles.

Brand ads will also cost you more, so you'll want to monitor them closely. Whether you're running keyword brand ads or product-based ads, the top of the Amazon search is prime real estate and, therefore, a pricier endeavor

UNDERSTANDING BUYING HABITS IS CRUCIAL TO THE SUCCESS OF YOUR ADS

Regardless of what you're advertising on Amazon, it's important to understand your readers' buying habits. Readers who buy only eBooks won't be persuaded to buy print if it's not what they're accustomed to purchasing. By the same token, readers who buy books in print aren't likely to switch to eBooks.

I mention this here because while you're starting your ads and searching for books for your keyword or product placement ads, be sure to find ones for the formats your reader prefers. In general, genre fiction tends to be heavily eBook-driven, whereas business books and literary fiction tend to be print book-focused.

Not sure which format resonates most with your readership? You can start by doing Amazon research and comparing sales ranks of print vs. eBook on the book page itself. Check out the top titles in your market and see which sales rank seems to be lower (lower indicates more sales, whereas a higher sales rank means fewer sales).

You can also look at their also-boughts to get a sense of preferred book formats, as well as popular books in your genre or niche.

Buying habits matter, especially with book formats, because by default Amazon will show your book ads regardless of format. And yes, if someone likes your book and clicks through to see if you have a format they want, that works, too. But format matters, especially with Kindle Unlimited, which many genre fiction fans prefer. When you're pulling together your product ads, you'll have a smattering of categories that you dump into markets, regardless of format preferences, but you also have the option of adding ASINs

(Amazon's version of ISBN for eBooks). It takes a bit more work, but it's worth it.

HOW MANY ADS SHOULD YOU RUN?

One theory encourages authors to run many, many ads. Some people profess that running dozens of ads really makes a difference but, let me tell you, it does not.

A few years ago, someone from Google Ads told me that running multiple ads (with likely the same keywords) hurts your overall ad visibility and can be very costly because you're essentially bidding against yourself for your ads. If you can run multiple ads with different keywords, that is okay, but in most cases, if you're running ads with 100 to 300 keywords, you'll get tapped out of options very quickly.

Ideally, I'd recommend running a keyword-targeting and product-targeting campaign, so at least two ads. You can run more, and if you have more books, you can run them on every book you have, provided the book is still relevant to the reader. You don't want to be bidding against yourself for keywords or products.

Keep in mind that your ads will need managing, so if you are running 50 different ads, you'll spend a great deal of time managing them. My suggestion? Start with three: keyword, product, and automatic.

The other reason to start with three types is that you never know which one will be stickier. Sometimes automatic ads do extremely well (though they have to be managed very carefully, which we'll discuss in a moment), and other times product ads end up being the best type to run. If you start with all three, you can get a good sense of what works and what doesn't for your particular book.

FINDING GREAT KEYWORD STRINGS FOR YOUR AMAZON ADS

Whether for sponsored product ads or brand ads, knowing how to find good keywords is the key to any successful ad run. Of all the things you do related to setting up your ads, finding good keywords will take you the most time. The good news: once you find some good keyword strings, you can probably keep running them for as long as you run your ads while still adding to them as your campaign progresses.

HOW MANY KEYWORDS SHOULD YOU HAVE?

To start, I'd recommend 300 to 400 keywords/keyword strings. I know this seems like a lot, but there are some easy and fun short-cuts for collecting them that I'll share with you later. Why so many? Because you want to cast your net wide. But as your campaign ages, you won't need to monitor each of these keywords; in fact as I take you through my process, you'll see that you end up moni-toring only 10 to 25 keywords.

Finding keyword strings isn't as hard as you might think. If you've read the chapters about Amazon keyword strings, you know I like to focus on supply and demand—specifically, high demand, low supply.

One of the biggest problems authors face when choosing keyword strings for their book page or their Amazon ads is choosing words that have very little search momentum or, conversely, are far too competitive. An example is "contemporary romance" for a romance novel.

The other consideration is how your consumer searches. As we've discussed, consumers search based on their needs. If you have a book about gluten intolerance, your consumer may search for "wheat allergies" because they're coming at this topic from their pain points, not yours. For the purpose of simplifying keyword strings, this chapter will be divided into two sections: keyword strings for fiction and keyword strings for nonfiction.

UNDERSTANDING THE DIFFERENT KEYWORD MATCH TYPES

Match types are exactly what the name implies: the type of match you want to pull up based on the keyword. Currently Amazon offers broad, phrase, and exact keyword matches.

Match types will pull in different audiences, so it's important to understand the distinction before you jump into adding your keyword strings. There is a shortcut around this, as I'll soon show you.

For now, let's see what each type means.

Broad Match Search: This is the most flexible of keyword match types; it allows your keyword to show up in a variety of forms. For example, let's say your keyword is "Star Wars." Your ad could show up for searches including the phrases "Star Wars movie," "Star Wars book," or "Star Wars T-shirt." Conversely, it could also show up for "the movie Star Wars," "book Star Wars," and so on. Broad gives you flexibility, but you're also casting a wide net, which may work in some instances, but could also start adding up in terms of paying for clicks on keyword terms that aren't related to you at all. An example of this would be using "Star Wars T-shirt" if all you have to offer is a book. Why? Because if a consumer is typing in "Star Wars T-shirt" they likely aren't a book buyer, so keep that in mind when you opt for Broad Match.

Phrase Match Search: This is a bit less flexible but still broad enough to pull in a good number of searches. Phrase match allows you to narrow your search terms using specific phrases. The key feature with this match type is that it allows you to control the word order. This helps to eliminate searches where a reader inserts a word (like "used") in between your keyword strings. However, it will include words before or after your keyword phrase. While it's similar to broad match, it still keeps the search within your target market. If you have keyword strings like "Star Wars book," your ad won't show in searches for T-shirts, mouse pads, or any other Star Wars paraphernalia.

Exact Match Search: This is the most limited of the search terms, which may seem unfavorable. There are phrases that certainly can work well within the parameters of specific words. You should know that using exact match will limit your options, which may be acceptable depending on what you're trying to accomplish. For example, using "Star Wars books" as a keyword will bring up searches for "Star Wars book" but not "book Star Wars."

WHICH MATCH TYPE IS RIGHT FOR YOUR AD CAMPAIGN?

The short answer is, Try them all.

The long answer is a bit more involved and, frankly, in nearly all of the ads I run, I add the keyword strings and experiment with different match types. I'll add each set of keyword strings and then isolate each by Phrase, Exact, and Broad match. That way I can see which keyword strings do better in terms of each match type. This approach is one of the most effective shortcuts to finding keywords:

find 100 to 200 and then rate them under each match type because you never know what'll stick.

In some cases, like author names, you may not want to use broad match because if you have too much "other" stuff, like a nonbook product, you could wind up in too many nonrelevant searches. But you can start with saving these names using all the matches and see which search term makes you money vs. which one costs you money.

AUTHOR NAMES AND BOOK TITLES AS KEYWORD STRINGS

Using author names and book titles is still a recommended strategy, though I use it more for fiction than nonfiction. As you experiment, you may find that the broad match isn't the best match type for names, but this does vary. This concept will appear later in the Understanding Amazon Ad Metrics chapter.

Be careful using book titles that are too similar to other books not related to your topic.

AMAZON'S KEYWORD SUGGESTIONS

Initially Amazon's suggestions aren't helpful, but at some point, they start improving. Generally around the 10-day mark, the ad algorithm kicks in and the keyword suggestions improve.

When you're adding keywords into your dashboard, you'll see Amazon's auto-complete pop up. Pay close attention because it could offer some insights into the keywords you will want to use in addition to those you already have used. Keyword suggestions and auto-complete are two different concepts, and I'm not sure why one is more accurate, but I've played with the auto-complete and I really like some of the keywords I'm offered!

NEGATIVE KEYWORD TARGETING

One of the best-kept secrets of Amazon ads is negative targeting. This can help pave a better road for your ads and increase the likelihood of a buy. It helps to narrow your search so you avoid spending money on keywords, books, and categories that aren't working for you. Negative keyword targeting is especially helpful for fiction authors. Let's say you have a Christian romance book you're eager to promote. Your readers don't want to be shown titles related to erotic romance. Therefore, you may want to include "sexy romance" or "erotic romance" as negative keywords so you don't waste money turning up in those searches. Conversely, if you have an erotic romance, you probably don't want to show up under a sweet or Christian romance search.

Science fiction also has numerous microgenres to which you'll want to be sensitive, so it's helpful if you're hyperfocused on any nuances or subgenre that isn't appropriate for your book or your target reader.

Even nonfiction is impacted by negative keywords, depending on the book topic. Your book may appeal to a specific niche, like beginning investors, so adding words like "seasoned investor" to your negative keywords dashboard might be appropriate.

At a minimum, I recommend also including the term "free" in your negative keywords list so you aren't coming up in searches for free eBooks. You'll also want to keep an eye on your dashboard to see what's pulling in traffic and what's wasting money. You can always add to your negative keyword dashboard. We'll dig into that as we start to unpack the Amazon "Search Terms."

FINDING KEYWORD STRINGS FOR NONFICTION

Amazon's new ad system radically changed how we search for nonfiction keyword strings, and it's become much more aligned with Google searches so, to a large degree, you can use Google to find your keyword strings.

If you've ever run a Google ad campaign, you're probably already familiar with its Keyword Planner tool, but if you're not, it's very easy to use. You could also use any keyword planner tool you have access to, even Ubersuggest, which is free. We use this one often to define keywords for our website, so it's a great way to start researching keywords to find the ones that will most resonate with your readers.

I want to examine the needs of readers when I'm searching for keyword strings for Amazon. Earlier in this book I described finding keyword strings for an Amazon optimization I did for a book on breathing better and I also discussed how *the reader is searching for the problem*, not the issue itself.

The same is true for your ads. Though "breathing better" should definitely be one of your keyword strings, you'll also want to add the readers' pain points to your list, which means you need to learn what's bringing them to your book. If you don't know this, play around with your preferred keyword tool, or start doing a search on Amazon and see what pops up. You'll quickly discover what's being purchased and what isn't.

Unlike recommendations in previous editions of this book, your ad keywords research will need to very closely match your book keywords. You'll want to find keyword strings and books that have a good sales rank. By "good" I mean 50,000 or lower.

Let's look at the keyword string "planning for retirement." This keyword string follows what I've talked about previously: supply and demand. Very little supply and the sales rank of the books shows a reasonably high demand:

1-16 of over 8,000 results for "planning for retirement"

Though 8,000 may seem like a high number, it's really not. There are some eight million books on Amazon (the exact number is not known, because Amazon does not release its data publicly), so 8,000 results for a popular money topic isn't bad. Check out some of the sales ranks of the books that populated under this search string:

Product details

Publisher : Houndstooth Press (April 23, 2021)

Language : English

Paperback : 124 pages

ISBN-10 : 1544516835

ISBN-13 : 978-1544516837

Item Weight : 5.9 ounces

Dimensions : 5.5 x 0.31 x 8.5 inches

Best Sellers Rank: #18,114 in Books (See Top 100 in Books)
   #41 in Retirement Planning (Books)

   #76 in Budgeting & Money Management (Books)

   #544 in Success Self-Help

Customer Reviews: ★★★★☆ ˅   254 ratings

Product details

ASIN : B084GB3GT9

Publisher : Adams Media; Updated edition (May 11, 2021)

Publication date : May 11, 2021

Language : English

File size : 3742 KB

Text-to-Speech : Enabled

Enhanced typesetting : Enabled

X-Ray : Enabled

Word Wise : Enabled

Sticky notes : On Kindle Scribe

Print length : 237 pages

Page numbers source ISBN : 144056972X

Best Sellers Rank: #55,535 in Kindle Store (See Top 100 in Kindle Store)

#9 in Personal Budgeting

#18 in Retirement Planning (Kindle Store)

#18 in Personal Money Management (Kindle Store)

Customer Reviews: ★★★★☆ ˅   643 ratings

AMAZON'S KEYWORD SUGGESTIONS FOR NONFICTION

Previous versions of the AMS dashboard have offered an unimpressive list of keyword suggestions, and it still does. While the initial batch of keyword suggestions remains unimpressive, they do get better as your ad ages because keyword suggestions improve as Amazon learns your ad. When you're setting up your ad, you certainly want to consider them, but if you check the keyword suggestions again in seven to ten days, you'll see a vast improvement.

USING AUTHOR NAMES AND BOOK TITLES

The previous example ("planning for retirement") showed a keyword string I'd absolutely add to my ads dashboard, but it also unearthed books I'd add, too. Your keywords should be a healthy blend of keyword strings, book titles, and author names. How many of each is hard to predict, meaning there isn't an exact metric saying "20% of this and 50% of that." The exact blend will depend on how your ad does with each set.

USING ALSO-BOUGHTS, AKA MORE ITEMS TO EXPLORE

Much like with the optimization chapters, you can absolutely use also-boughts (which I've noticed are gradually being renamed "More Items to Explore") as part of your keyword strings (book titles and authors). Just remember the same rules apply: make sure the sales rank is solid.

FINDING KEYWORD STRINGS FOR GENRE FICTION

Genre fiction always seems more successful when you use other author names and book titles, so let's start there. Again, just as I advised in the nonfiction guidance, you'll want to look for searches that are pulling in lots of traffic and authors who are selling lots of books. A sales rank of 50,000 or less is great—but obviously the lower the number, the better.

An easy way to get started is to grab authors from keyword searches; again, for genre fiction, it's important to be specific. Readers who love time travel may not want a time travel romance, and there's a distinct difference between these readers and these genres.

You can start on the bestseller lists, and delve into these titles and authors. But you can also go into the also-boughts/more items to explore list and start grabbing some books and authors from there.

Basically, I'm going to start with these authors, using their names and book titles, and start building my keyword strings list. Just click on any author to pull up their page and a list of their books. Then start taking notes!

Remember, you can also use the keywords you developed in your optimization, so add those to the list. And speaking of keyword strings. I've talked a lot about author names and book titles, but keyword strings are equally important. I recommend you find some in addition to what you used for your book optimization.

Seasonal keywords are another fun element you can add. For example: *summer romance read, tax time help, summer beach read, sweet holiday romance, small town holiday romance*. Add them during the appropriate season and remove them when the season is over!

KEYWORD STRINGS FOR MEMOIRS, LITERARY FICTION, WOMEN'S FICTION

These keyword strings will fall into the same bucket as just mentioned, except you might be more inclined to pull in keyword strings that readers are using in their searches. For example, in the case of a memoir about Alzheimer's, you might use the word "Alzheimer's" in your keyword.

CHILDREN'S FICTION, YOUNG ADULT FICTION

Much as with other fiction, your keyword strings for children's and young adult books may be better served by a blend of author titles and solutions. For example, a children's book on kindness might benefit from the keyword string "teaching children kindness."

Some keyword experts like to talk about doubling up keywords —for example, the term "book book book" is really popular on Amazon, because of ... well, books. But using that one won't get you a good return on your ads. Instead, consider doubling up on keywords that are performing. For example, if "book marketing" is performing, I'd do a keyword string that reads "book marketing book marketing." It doesn't work in every case, but try it and see how the keywords do!

ONE FINAL NOTE ABOUT KEYWORD STRINGS

When you include book titles, I recommend staying away from one-word titles. I haven't personally achieved an affordable cost per click (CPC) by using them. For example, "hot" or "smokin'," which you tend to see a lot in romance, are probably too broad and won't get you a worthwhile result in search. Worse, it may be costly and yield little in sales.

ADDING KEYWORD STRINGS TO YOUR ADS

The final step is adding your keyword strings to your ad. Add them manually since uploading an Excel file never seems to work. As you'll see, the Match Types are already checked for you, so when you add your keywords you don't have to re-add them under the various match types, which makes it easy.

PRODUCT TARGETING ADS

Product targeting is exactly what the name says: you're targeting other, similar books in your market. You're finding specific books, authors, and categories to align with.

To get started, be very clear on your genre; for example, if you want to align your book with successful women's fiction titles but your book is really more contemporary romance, your ads won't do well at all. In fact, misaligning your products (or even your keywords when doing keyword ads) can dramatically impact the cost of your ad and the relevancy of your entire campaign. But if you're already running a successful keyword campaign and have your author names and book titles, that's a good place to start. And here's a tip: as you're locating books to pair your ad with, remember the reader preferences I mentioned earlier. Are you showing your ad by eBook searches or print searches? This matters to your reader and their buying habits.

SETTING UP PRODUCT TARGETING ADS

Since the setup dashboard is the same for keyword or product targeting, just pick Product Targeting under the Targeting options. When you do, it flips the bidding area to Categories and Individual Products.

I used to like adding categories to these ads as well as products (which you can do from the same dashboard), but Amazon has changed how categories show up in search, so be mindful that while adding them can't hurt your campaign, they may not drive a lot of results. But this is a great opportunity to add book titles and authors!

How many do you need? Consider starting with 25 to 50 and keep adding from there. You don't need as many to start with as you do keywords because keywords have to be managed more carefully, and not all keywords will work well, as I explained in the previous chapter.

You may be thinking at this point that product targeting sounds much easier than keywords. It is, but it doesn't work well for all books.

Mine, for example, do much better with keyword targeting. This is partly because there aren't many books on book marketing—none that are new, anyway. It depends on the book and the genre.

I always run the product targeting ads alongside my keyword ads because things change on Amazon so you never know.

Remember, the most important consideration on Amazon is that your book aligns with the right genre, keywords, and target market.

A FINAL NOTE ON PRODUCT TARGETING ADS

If your book matches with a nonbook product, there's no reason you can't advertise alongside it. For example, if you have a Star Wars-related book, you could advertise alongside the release of the latest Star Wars movie. Or if you have a fun book about kids making Christmas decorations, you could advertise it next to Christmas stuff, decorating, or whatever. Also, consider running your holiday romance advertising next to a Hallmark movie or something similar!

Consider book pairing, when appropriate. It's fun to explore and you can add the nonbook product into your ads dashboard just like you add books!

AMAZON BRAND ADS

When Amazon brand ads were made available to all authors, it was a true game-changer. As I have noted, the ads show up at the top of search. Here's a sampling of what they look like:

FBI mystery thriller that's a must read...
Shop Elle Gray Books ›

The 7 She Saw (Blake Wilder FBI Mystery Thriller Book 1)
★★★★☆ 7,623

A Perfect Wife (Blake Wilder FBI Mystery Thriller Book 2)
★★★★☆ 7,010

Her Perfect Crime (Blake Wilder FBI Mystery Thriller Book 3)
★★★★☆ 6,185

Brand ads are set up in the same Amazon ads dashboard as the sponsored products. Just click Continue under sponsored brands to get started.

Choose your campaign type

View drafts

Sponsored Products

Sponsored Brands

Lockscreen Ads

Promote products to shoppers actively searching with related keywords or viewing similar products on Amazon.

Help shoppers discover your brand and products on Amazon with rich, engaging creatives.

These ads are based on shoppers' interests and are shown when they 'unlock' their Kindle E-readers or Fire Tablets to begin reading or shopping for books.

Continue

Continue

Continue

Explore Sponsored Products

Sponsored Brands eligibility

Explore Lockscreen Ads

Once you're there, you'll see a dashboard that's very similar to the sponsored products one. Select your three (or more) books and start to work on the creative.

With sponsored products, you can add any ad copy; with brand ads, you don't have that option, but your creative copy is also very short. You're limited to 50 characters so writing the copy can be challenging. You'll want to spend some time on this copy.

Another piece of the ad set up is your author photo, which as of this writing does not automatically populate. Just upload the one you used for your Amazon Author Central account.

If you click on the Products tab, you'll see the books you have listed for your brand ad and can reshuffle them from there. This is particularly important if you've written a series and want the titles to show up in order.

RUNNING SUCCESSFUL BRAND ADS

I love doing brand ads, but they are more expensive than your regular sponsored products. The top of the Amazon search page doesn't come cheap! Be mindful that, much like in sponsored products, the number of reviews and your average star-rating will show up in the banner, so if your books don't have reviews, or you have a low star rating (three-star and below) you may want to skip brand ads altogether. Books that do well in brand ads tend to be those with a robust four-star and above rating so keep that in mind if you're considering advertising books that aren't selling well.

AMAZON'S AUTOMATIC ADS

Since the setup for automatic ads is pretty intuitive, I won't go into the details of setup. It is worth mentioning, though, that automatic ads, while seemingly easy, can eat up your entire budget if you aren't careful.

Much as with all of the Amazon ad offerings, automatic ads align with the book algorithm, keywords, categories, and overall placement on Amazon. Therefore, if your book isn't optimized, if it's not readily showing up in search, or if it's showing up under the wrong keywords, your automatic ads won't do well at all.

This is worth repeating: Automatic targeting is when the Amazon algorithm takes over, and if you've done nothing to optimize your book, your ads may end up being a bit of a free-for-all.

That said, automatic ads can be an easy way to get started with the ads system and, if the book is optimized, can be very effective for you. And it's worth mentioning again to be mindful of your budget because, like brand ads, automatic ads can eat up your entire ads budget if they aren't monitored carefully.

MANAGING YOUR AMAZON ADS

ow that you understand how to set up ads, and find keywords and categories, let's talk about some strategies to help make your ads more profitable.

KILLING OFF KEYWORDS: WHEN TO DO IT AND WHY

Remember when I talked about Amazon's relevancy score? Keywords, for obvious reasons, factor heavily into this, so don't hesitate to kill off keywords that are draining your budget. How soon should you kill them off? I'd allow five to seven days for the ads to gain some traction and start pausing after that.

COPYING AN AD CAMPAIGN

I've run ads for my books that do extremely well, and I often copy them so I don't have to start from scratch. However, there's a downside. Any optimization or algorithm boost associated with the ad set won't carry over; at least, that's been my experience.

Copying an ad set is a quick and easy way to kick-start another campaign but, in terms of ad algorithm, you're starting over.

Is it ever a bad idea to copy an ad set and the associated keywords? Yes, if the ad set was bad, copying it over and giving it new life is unlikely to change how the ad works. If it didn't work well in the past, there was something inherently wrong with either the keywords or the ad itself.

AD START AND END DATES

Be mindful of ad start and end dates. Unless you're running ads to support a specific effort such as a price discount that expires on a certain date, keep the end date open. If the ad isn't effective, you can always kill it. But you don't want an ad that's doing well to end, so leave it open-ended.

You'll see some high bids in there, and it's surprising when you think of paying $1.84 for "book marketing," for example. But if you're in the fiction genre, it's much higher. We manage ad campaigns for some of our romance authors, and I see $5 and $6 a click, so you'll want to watch the bids closely.

What I've found is that as the Amazon system "learns" your book, the bids will change, often for the better (lower) but sometimes, they'll be higher. That is why you want to watch these ads over the first week, which is when a lot of your bid adjustments will happen.

MEASURING THE EFFECTIVENESS OF YOUR ADS

Before we get into bids, CPC, CTR, and the rest, let's talk about measuring the profitability of your ads. Since it is hard to measure the effectiveness directly, it's important to start with a baseline. How much are you selling without any kind of ad support? If your book is in Kindle Unlimited, how many page reads are you getting? Make a note of this number because as we'll see in a minute, the Amazon Ads dashboard leaves a lot to be desired.

AMAZON'S SUGGESTED BIDS

Amazon's suggested bids are a good metric to follow, so I'd recommend going with those bids initially and then watching them closely as your ad set ages. Often the suggestions will change, up or down, so stay on top of the bids. Again, it's important to watch them while Amazon "learns" your ad set.

PROFITABILITY OF YOUR KEYWORD STRINGS

Sometimes keyword strings start strong and then drop off. When that happens, I recommend raising your bid on that keyword and watching the results. It may be that the bid isn't high enough to keep pulling in readers. Raising your keyword bid could net you more exposure, by landing you higher on the book search page or making you one of the first books shown in the carousel on the book page.

The other reason for the drop-off could be that interest in the topic has subsided. I often see this with trendy topics and keyword strings that mirror newsy, pop culture, or seasonally focused books.

By the same token, if you see a keyword that's getting clicks but no tangible sales, I'd pause it because it means you're wasting your money.

Running Amazon ads may also mean keeping track of peak sales periods. We know from research that books peak in sales around holidays like Christmas, and book sales are better in winter than summer, but events like the mass quarantine of 2020 may skew that data.

In other words, while the holidays are a great time for promotions and ads, boosting them during a major national event might be advantageous as well. Big weather events also have this impact. Super-hot days or frigid winter weather that keeps folks inside can do the same thing for books sales as holidays. Generally, book sales go down during election cycles (November for the US market), but be mindful that a lot of people are "done" with all the political noise out there and may want to escape into a book!

BOOSTING YOUR AMS CAMPAIGNS

In the testing I've done, I've found that for genre fiction in particular, doing ads on books that aren't part of the Kindle Unlimited program doesn't work as well as it does for the books in KDP Select, which are always part of this program. Why? Many fiction readers in Kindle Unlimited get book recommendations from these ads, and although you may not see it in direct book sales, you'll see it in page reads in Kindle Unlimited.

Books in a series, which includes multiple books about a theme, also tend to increase your overall sales. For example, let's say you write about saving money, starting a business, or parenting. Having multiple books out, even if you're running ads for only one of them, will help with your overall exposure and potentially increase sales of other books because you're attracting more readers.

Another way to boost your Amazon ads is by adding the ad keyword strings to your book page, in your book description or any enhanced content you can include via Amazon Author Central. If you can include a keyword or two in your subtitle, even better. Keep in mind that your Amazon page is "spidered," much like your website is spidered by Google. "Spidered" means located, indexed, and networked to other books and search strings consumers may pop into the Amazon search bar. Having ad keyword strings on your book page is not only a great idea; it's mandatory if you want to get a good bounce from your ads.

WRITING A GREAT BOOK AD

t's not easy to create an impactful ad working with only 150 characters. Most of us are very good at writing pages of text; having to edit what we have to say down to just 150 characters is much harder.

I recommend doing some searches on your keywords to see what kind of ads pop up. What piques your interest? Take a screenshot of the ads that make you want to learn more. You aren't going to copy the ads, but let them inspire you to write your own. It's a great exercise to ensure you understand what inspires a click and what might fall flat with your reader.

ADDING KEYWORD STRINGS TO ADS

Yes, you can add keyword strings to ads but only if it makes sense for your ad copy, particularly because you have very limited ad space. In many cases, it may be easier for nonfiction authors to do this than it is for fiction authors.

RUNNING ADS WITHOUT AD COPY

Amazon now gives you the option to run book ads without copy, which allows you to promote multiple books in one ad. While I've seen ad copy make a difference, I've also seen cases where it doesn't matter, and this is often where and how your ad is shown— on a search page rather than on the actual book page. Amazon can sometimes show your ad without ad copy, even if you included it when you created the ad. There's also some data to suggest that a reader is more swayed by the number of reviews, the book cover, and the price than anything else. You may want to try two ad sets, one with copy and one without, and see which does better for you.

CREATING MULTIPLE ADS TO SERVE DIFFERENT MARKETS

I always try to use keywords for the nonfiction books we manage. You can also use keywords specific to the various benefits of the book.

Let's say your book fits in a few categories, which most books do. For example, you might have a book about growing a new business, gluten intolerance, or food allergies. Each of these topics has a subset of interests that you probably found in your book research; each subset can be incorporated into your ad sets.

For example, let's say you have a book about fatigue and there's a chapter or perhaps an entire section on Lyme disease, which tends to peak in the summer months. You might consider running ads geared to the topic of Lyme disease only during a certain time of year.

Whatever keywords you're using for your ads, use them whenever possible on your Amazon book page, too. Whether it's in the book description or your author interview, sprinkling them throughout your book page can help with ad relevancy. I recommend monitoring your ads until you've found the handful of keyword strings that are really helping to push sales and use those!

UNDERSTANDING AMAZON
AD TERMINOLOGY

We're going to dig into all of the Amazon ads metrics in the next chapter, but this is a good place to pause and discuss some of the terminology you'll see in the Amazon ads system.

CTR – Click-through Rate

This might be the most talked about metric on the Amazon ad dashboard. Why? Because it means your ad is drawing people to your book page. The higher the CTR, in theory, the better your ad is doing. But many bloggers neglect to mention that a high CTR isn't a high sales number. In fact, you could have a high CTR and no sales, and that's a problem.

What's an ideal CTR? Well, 100% is obviously your target, but that's not always possible. Generally, 0.5% and higher is a good place to be. The average click-through rate for search engines is 2.7%, so anything higher than 0.5% is great, certainly, but if you aren't selling books, you're getting yourself into a sticky situation. Amazon won't keep showing an ad that isn't selling books. That's where your ad relevancy comes in.

CVR – Conversion Rate

CVR is the ratio of clicks to orders. The fewer clicks required to generate a single sale, the better. That is what Amazon looks for. By the same token, if your conversion rate is low (meaning you need more clicks to close a sale), your ads will cost you more because it takes more clicks to make a sale.

ACoS – Advertising Cost of Sale

Let me say up front, this metric can be confusing or inaccurate. The ads dashboard isn't measuring all of your sales, and we'll dig into that in a minute. The other piece is that ACoS often lags, sometimes as much as 10 days, behind your ads. If you're looking for real-time data, this isn't it.

Impressions

The number of impressions is how many times your ad has been shown on the Amazon website; this covers search page results as well as the ad being shown on individual retail pages.

Clicks

The number of times your ad has been clicked.

CPC – Cost per Click

An average of how much you are paying for each click on your ad.

UNDERSTANDING AMAZON AD METRICS

The Amazon Ads system offers a great deal of reporting, but only some of it is useful. I know many of you will just stop reading here. Let's face it: most of us hate math. I'll try to stay out of the weeds when it comes to ad metrics because they don't really matter. Yes, your CTR matters, absolutely. But ACoS (average cost of sales) is a bit of a mess, and knowing your impressions is only helpful as it relates to your overall ad visibility. Otherwise, impressions are just, well, impressions.

For all of this to make sense, we have to dig into the only things that matter. If you want to read about Amazon reports and get deep in the weeds on that, there are a lot of other Amazon books that will help you do that. But for this chapter, we're going to focus on the stuff that (in my opinion) truly matters.

UNDERSTANDING YOUR CONVERSION RATE

A CVR is the number of clicks it takes before you sell a book. But let me stress that there is no standard for your CVR; it depends on several factors. Let me give you an example.

Let's say your book costs $7.50, and your keyword costs you

$0.75. You must sell one book for every 10 clicks for this to make sense, but even that doesn't take into account Amazon's cut on your book. So let's do this again. Let's say your cut, after Amazon takes its share, is $3. Now you need to sell one book for every four clicks. That ups the ad game considerably.

What's a good/average conversion rate? As the example above shows, a good CVR for one author may not work for another. Still, most experts agree that 20 clicks to get one order is a good place to start.

How can you improve your CVR? Sit tight, because we'll cover that a bit later in the book.

One note on CVR: if your books are in Kindle Unlimited, you'll want to keep tabs on your page reads because books that are "loaned" aren't reflected in your CVR. But they may be reflected in your CTR, which we'll look at next.

MANAGING YOUR CLICK-THROUGH RATE

This is really the heartbeat of any campaign. Your CTR is key to how well your ads are doing, i.e., how many times people see your ad compared with how often they click it. Impressions tell you if your ad is delivering, but your CTR tells you if readers are taking notice and are interested enough to click.

If your book is in Kindle Unlimited and you tend to get more page reads than actual sales, this CTR number is golden for you. But as I've mentioned, keep an eye on your page reads because that will impact how well your book ads are doing. While page reads are now reported on the dashboard, this data is often incorrect and it isn't in real time, whereas your KDP sales dashboard is.

If your click-through rate isn't great, do whatever you can to improve it because the higher your click-through rate, the less your ads will cost you.

Are Your Ads Relevant?

Relevancy is the all-important element of Amazon's search algorithm and ads. If you are selecting keywords or categories that aren't relevant to your actual market, your CTR will reflect this. In other words, your ads aren't relevant to the market you are serving them to. In the next chapter, we'll explain this in detail but if you're running ads that aren't seeing a decent CTR, consider pausing them until you can fix the keywords, products, or categories.

ABOUT YOUR AMAZON ADS BUDGET

Ironically, it's hard to get Amazon to spend your total budget. You aren't paying for impressions; you're paying for clicks. When I work with authors to manage their ads, I encourage them to start with a $20 daily budget and I always suggest running three ads. I get a lot of pushback on that because as the authors are doing math in their head, a $20 daily budget across three ads can get unruly very fast, but for 99% of the ads I manage, it doesn't. Amazon doesn't spend your money that fast; in fact sometimes it's hard to get Amazon to spend your daily budget in a week. That's great news, certainly, but it doesn't mean Amazon ads are inexpensive. As we've discussed, sometimes you can spend a lot of money on ads that don't get any sales. But if you're still nervous about your daily budget, I recommend a budget cap, which is easy to add. We'll discuss that next.

AMAZON AD PORTFOLIOS AND PORTFOLIO BUDGETS

When I manage an author's ads, I always create a portfolio so I can click on that tab and go straight to the ads I'm managing. This is particularly helpful when I'm working on a campaign where the author is also running his own set of ads. Within that portfolio you can set an overall monthly budget, so you can cap it at, let's say, $200 or $300, depending on your comfort level. If you're doing this right, it's hard to run through your daily ad spend, but setting a budget is still a sound safeguard if you're running multiple ads on various platforms and want to keep a tight rein on your overall ad budget.

HOW DO I KNOW IF I'M MAKING MONEY?

Since I've been discussing metrics, it's worth mentioning that before you start your ads, you should take note of your royalties and page reads (if you're in Kindle Unlimited). Since the reporting on the Amazon dashboard is delayed, it's good to know where you stand before you launch a campaign.

Additionally, if you have multiple books or books in a series, take note of those sales. A consumer lands on your book page, notes your other titles, and decides to grab one of your earlier books, so it's worth paying attention to that as well!

THE HIDDEN POWER OF SEARCH TERMS

ne of the best ways to manage your ads is to pave a better pathway. By this, I mean get your ads more focused. For this reason, I have given the topic of search terms its own chapter.

When you first run your ads, you'll start with 300 to 400 keywords, which you now know how to find. Although you'll put in some good efforts, not all of these keywords will be viable. In other words, even though you have an ad set with 400 keywords, you aren't managing all 400 of them every time you open up your dashboard.

WHY SEARCH TERMS MATTER

When you first put your book up on Amazon, your search terms will be blank. There's nothing to show yet. But as your book ad ages and is shown to more people, search terms become a valuable asset to the success of your campaign.

Running Amazon ads is like getting on an eight-lane freeway. You don't want to use all eight lanes because that traffic may not be the traffic you actually want to your Amazon retail page. By narrowing the lanes, by creating a more focused path, you'll start to bring in more targeted traffic and, consequently, start converting more consumers into buyers.

It's also a great way to get a sense of your customer's behavior and the keywords they're using to find your book. As we'll see in a minute, it's a fabulous way to generate more keyword ideas!

BEING MINDFUL OF RANDOM TRAFFIC

Let's say you've been running your ads for a while now (give it seven to ten days before making any big decisions!). You see that your impressions are very high and your CTR is high, but you're not selling books. Or at least, the ads dashboard isn't showing any book sales. Remember we talked about calculating all of your sales, not just what's being reported on the ads dashboard.

Here's what's happening: You literally send all the traffic to your Amazon book page. Basically, you're throwing stuff against the wall, hoping that some of it sticks. What happens in this case is problematic.

First, if Amazon sees that your book isn't selling for the ads it is serving up, Amazon will start to show your book less. Consequently, your ads are going to cost you more money. The other thing this tells Amazon is that your book isn't relevant to the reader. Now, this could have to do with your book page, but it could also have to do with your keywords. That's why it bears repeating that relevant keywords are paramount to the success of your ad campaign. You may want to come up under "all things thriller and mystery," but there is a lot of competition for that category. Also, are you sure that's your appropriate genre? As you'll see in a minute, search terms will show you where your book is showing up and where you might be wasting money.

SEARCH TERMS: THE SURPRISING SECRET THEY REVEAL

Not only are search terms helpful for narrowing your ads and ad spend, but they can also show you if your book is optimized correctly. If it's not, you'll struggle to get your ads to work well and get shown to the right people.

You can find the search terms once you click on the individual ad because they will show up for each of the ad types, even automatic ads.

Targeting

Negative targeting

Search terms

Creative

Budget rules

Campaign settings

History

Clicking on that will take you to all of the terms that customers popped in to get to your book. It will also show you what resulted in a click vs. what's just wasting your money. Sometimes odd connections will pop up; take a look at the arrow in the screenshot below. For this client I noticed that the keyword I had added, "Janet Evanovich," was pulling up some odd results. And that isn't the only example I found. Since there were no sales for that keyword, and it was pulling up a mishmash of keywords, I paused it.

Customer search term ⓘ	Keywords ⓘ	Match type ⓘ
Total: 273		
freida mcfadden books	freida mcfadden	Phrase
steamy murder mystery	mystery books	Broad
tempest island series jana deleon	jana deleon	Phrase
lethal bayou beauty by jana deleon	jana deleon	Broad
murder and the mermaid	murder of a mermaid	Exact
murder at the serpentine bridge by andrea penrose	murder at the serpentine bridge	Phrase
stephanie plum series	janet evanovich	Broad
1.99 mystery books	mystery books	Phrase
a bespoke murder	murder most english	Broad
a market for murder	murder most english	Broad
a village fete murder	a village fete murder	Exact
alice penny	lucy foley	Broad

Once I pull these reports for clients, I either add keywords (because these reports often spark great new keyword ideas), or I'll add a bunch to negative targeting if they are wasting the author's money. I do this weekly. If you do this consistently, you will find that the path to your ad becomes more focused and more profitable.

HACKING AMAZON'S AD SYSTEM

L et's start here: **Amazon Ads Do Not Sell Your Book – Your Book Sells Your Book**

In this section we're going to examine the factors that determine the success of your Amazon ads, but also your book on the Amazon site—because everything matters.

RELEVANCY MATTERS

At this point you're probably sick of hearing the word "relevancy," but most of Amazon's algorithm is this invisible. Amazon ads and your CTR are a great indication of your overall relevancy score on Amazon, particularly with your Amazon ads.

Too often I see authors picking book titles, keywords, and categories that don't align with their book. Let me give you an example.

An author wanted me to look at the ads for her book. The book was romantic suspense with a psychic twist and a psychic protagonist. These were the markets she picked for the book:

- Romantic suspense

- Paranormal suspense
- Romantic thriller

However, when we looked through the other books nestled under the "paranormal suspense" genre on Amazon, they were different from the book she was promoting.

The keywords, products, and categories you pick for your book are extremely important to the overall success of your Amazon ad. But how well your book is optimized matters, too.

THE OPTIMIZATION OF YOUR BOOK ON AMAZON

There are numerous books and blogs that discuss the numbers you need to understand to get better results on the Amazon ads site, and while those are important, there's more to the Amazon ads than just the metrics. If you're looking at your ACoS and thinking, "Wow, I'm losing money on these ads," you may be right, but you're likely wrong because the ACoS is so inaccurate. For this reason, I like to look at other factors—like how well your book is optimized on Amazon—that can impact how well your ads do.

Understanding why your ads aren't working is often a multi-level process. Many factors are involved in your overall Amazon ad success, and one of them is how well your book is optimized. When you uploaded your book to Amazon, did you get creative with your keywords? And how about your categories? Or are you like that romantic suspense author I just mentioned, sitting in the wrong category? If you aren't sure, go back through the optimization chapters and reevaluate where your book sits on the Amazon site and whether it's in the correct genre.

I'll leave you with this little nugget: of all of the book pages I evaluate and all the optimizations I do, 75% of authors are sitting in the wrong genre, using the wrong keywords, and aligning with the wrong categories.

Now, let's discuss what consumers see when they see your ad on Amazon.

FACTORS THAT MAY DISCOURAGE CONSUMERS FROM CLICKING YOUR AD

Let's assume your keywords are spot on and your categories are perfect for your book genre, yet your ads still aren't doing much. In fact, they're just costing you money. You're getting many impressions, but not a lot of click-throughs. And you know that the longer these ads run with high impressions and low clicks, the less likely Amazon is to keep showing them. But the reasons your ads aren't doing well may have nothing to do with the ad setup; in fact, it could have more to do with your book than anything else.

As we run through these factors, note that they are listed in order of importance to the reader.

Book cover: Any book on Amazon, whether in an ad or a search result, is defined by its book cover. Consumers decide whether they want to know more about your book based on the cover. "Judging a book by its cover" may seem shallow, but it's very true in publishing. Your cover can not only make or break your success on Amazon; it can also make or break the success of your ads.

Ask yourself: is my book cover strong enough for this genre? Could it stand beside every book on the bestseller list? If you answer "no" or "I'm not sure," you probably have some work to do.

Book title: Much like our book covers, we become emotionally tethered to our book titles. Anyone who dares suggest changing a book title should be banished! But titles, much like book covers, can make or break your book.

Consider these well-known books and their original titles:

First Impressions was the working title for *Pride and Prejudice*. And imagine if *The Great Gatsby* had been published under the original title, *Trimalchio in West Egg*. Yes, that's the absolute truth. And finally my personal favorite: *All's Well that Ends Well* was the original name for *War and Peace*.

Book reviews: Most people don't buy a book naked; a book with zero reviews does not have great appeal to the reader. Nor does an ad for a book with two and a half stars. While I'm not suggesting that you hold off doing ads until you have pages and pages of Amazon reviews, don't expect to run a profitable ad campaign with two so-so reviews. Generally, consumers are mistrustful of books that have endless five-star reviews. A nice balance is generally 4.5 overall (according to a study *USA Today* did several years ago). I recommend launching an ad campaign once you have 10 reviews.

Book pricing: All authors have invested a great deal in our books, and we certainly want to make money from them, but pricing them out of your market is a problem. Pricing your book competitively is important.

Kindle Unlimited for Fiction: Fiction books in general tend to do better with ads when they're in Kindle Unlimited. You may want to make your eBook exclusive to Amazon, but in testing we've done (along with the hundreds of campaigns we've managed) we've found that fiction, in particular, does better with Amazon ads when the book is in Kindle Unlimited. This may be a result of the reader audience being predisposed to getting books that are part of the Kindle Unlimited library, as well as the fact the Amazon algorithm also favors this.

Advertising copy: Shockingly, your ad copy is important but not vital to the success of your ads!

GOING DEEPER: WHAT FACTORS IMPACT CONVERSION RATE?

So, you've gotten readers to land on your book page, but how can you get them to click and buy? Here is a list of the features that readers pay attention to along with a map of where the eye tracks on the Amazon retail pages. I mentioned the Z pattern that reflects how all consumers scan websites, and this tracking map is a great indication of that:

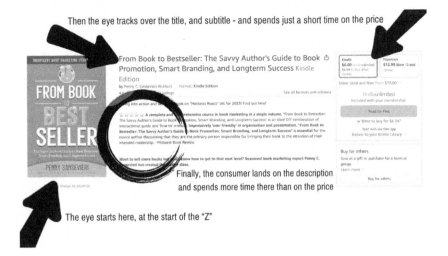

What factors encourage or discourage a buy? Here's the list:

- Book cover
- Product description
- Customer reviews
- Price
- Look inside
- Book formats

Amazon Ads Success Tip!

Book formats matter on Amazon. While I've discussed the importance of Kindle Unlimited for genre fiction authors, you should always have a print version of your book for the ads to do better. It can be paperback or hardback; it doesn't matter. But having multiple book formats will increase the likelihood of your ad being successful!

PART SIX
BONUS STRATEGIES, AUTHOR CENTRAL AND MORE!

HOW TO MAXIMIZE AMAZON AUTHOR CENTRAL

All Amazon authors, no matter when or what they've published, have an author page that shows up along with their books when you search for the author name on Amazon—*if they've claimed their pages.*

Surprisingly, many authors haven't claimed their pages. If you're not sure whether you've claimed yours, head over to https://author.amazon.com/. You can access it using your Amazon sign-in. Even if you're traditionally published, you can still have an Amazon author page.

To claim the page, you must sign in and add content to the page. Make sure all your books are claimed under your author page. It's easy enough. Simply list them in Author Central by inserting their ISBNs or ASINs and posting them to your page. Amazon will double-check your entries for accuracy. Once it does, you'll find a library of your books on your Author Central page.

In addition to your Amazon US page, you should also check out your international pages, which I'll cover in a minute!

GETTING STARTED WITH YOUR AUTHOR CENTRAL PAGE

If you're unfamiliar with Author Central, go to author.amazon.com and log in. You'll see a place to upload your author photo and bio and, as I just mentioned, you'll be able to grab your books, too.

Many authors who have published with a publisher (traditional or hybrid) think they don't have access to their Author Central page but that's not true. All authors, regardless of how they were published, have access to Author Central.

THE CHANGES TO AMAZON AUTHOR CENTRAL PAGES IN 2023

In case you haven't noticed, Author Central went through a major overhaul in late December of 2022. The ability to add blog updates and images or videos is now gone. (They may still show up on your international pages; the reason for this uncertainty is that Amazon is gradually shifting all of its Author Central pages to this new format, but the move for international pages will be slow.)

I thought it was a good time to explain how these changes might impact your book and author brand.

If you haven't already done so, go to your Author Central page and check out what it looks like now. Here is my before:

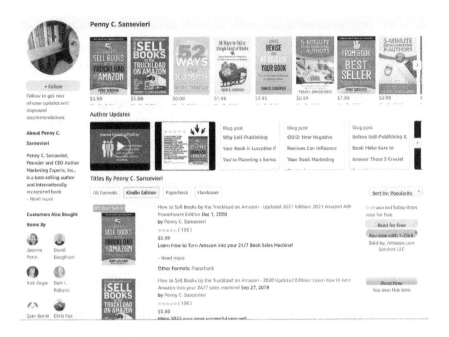

Here is what it looks like now:

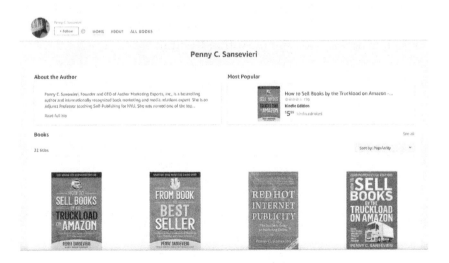

When Amazon changes any of its author-related benefits, it can be advantageous or not. Author Central pages get upwards of two million hits per year, so I suspect that Amazon got rid of the option to add a blog because some authors were adding their blogs but not keeping them up to date, which reflected poorly on the author, but also on the feature of being able to add your blog RSS feed to your author page.

The other piece Amazon eliminated was the ability to add images, which I loved. I suspect these changes were made because of the vetting required for blog feeds and images. After all, Amazon does monitor what it allows on its site.

Still, I wish the company had kept these options. I think they added to the whole "flavor" of your author page on Amazon, giving readers a better chance to get to know you.

Maybe, at some point Amazon will add these options back (and, as I said, they're still on the Amazon international author pages) but for now, let's explore one of the features Amazon has added to these newly designed author pages.

BOOK RECOMMENDATIONS

This is a brand-new feature, which is cool. You're able to push your own books as well as recommend someone else's. Here's what it looks like on the back end of Author Central:

Recommend books I have written

Use this section to tell your readers more about your books. These can help readers learn what makes these books special and help them decide what to read next.

My most talked about book is...	Select book
My book I wish more readers knew about is...	Select book
If you are new to my work, I recommend starting with my book...	Select book
If you want to get lost in a story, I recommend my book...	Select book

Recommend books by other authors

Use this section to share book recommendations to your readers for other books. These recommendations can be of books you think readers will like or books that have your stamp of approval.

If you like my work, I think you'll like...	Select book
A book I couldn't put down was...	Select book
A book that left an impression on me was...	Select book

Once it's filled in, here's what it looks like:

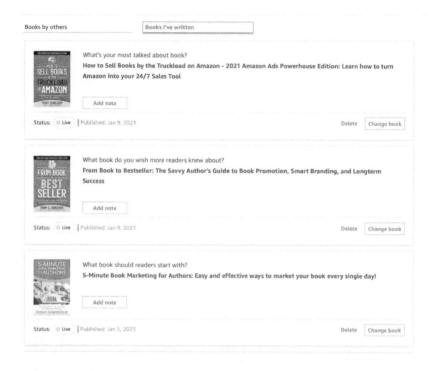

This is a good opportunity to highlight a book that's not getting enough play, but keep in mind how it shows up on your Amazon Author Central page, because that could influence which of your own books you decide to recommend.

Here is how it shows up on your Amazon Author Central page:

The first book in this list of titles is a book recommendation I added, which we'll discuss in a moment. But you have to scroll to get to my other recommendations. This is on page 2:

Penny C. Sansevieri's book recommendations

What book do you wish more readers knew about?
From Book to Bestseller: The Savvy Author's Guide to Book Promotio...
by Penny C. Sansevieri

What's your most talked about book?
How to Sell Books by the Truckload on Amazon - Updated 2021 Editio...
by Penny C. Sansevieri

What book should readers start with?
5-Minute Book Marketing for Authors: Easy and effective ways t...
by Penny C. Sansevieri

I love the idea of recommending other authors' books; it's a nice way to network with other authors. However, keep in mind that your book recommendations reflect on your brand, so be mindful that you recommend books that align with your genre and reader market.

Recommendations make for a nice networking opportunity, too. If you're in a group with authors or if you have authors with whom you've been networking, swapping out recommendations could be a nice way to network via Author Central; it's also a good way to thank people or show them some love on your Author Central pages. But you can also recommend your own books. And why not? Use these new Author Central features to your advantage. Experiment with them!

I think at some point Amazon will add to its Author Central pages. As I said, I'd love to see them add back some image and video options, but in the interim, keep in mind that you can always add video to your individual book pages via the Amazon upload feature. You can do this from your desktop or phone. Remember that you can only do a book at a time, so you can't upload a single video for all of your books at once.

CUSTOMIZE YOUR SHAREABLE AUTHOR URL

This isn't a new feature but definitely something you'll want to check out if you haven't already done so. Head over to author.amazon.com and click on Edit Profile, which takes you to the page where you can upload your author photo and bio. It's also the place where you can customize your shareable URL. Just click Edit and create it. This is a very effective way to create an easier pathway to your Author Central page and all your books!

Author Page URL

Currently only available for your Amazon.com Author Page

Copy the text below to share your author page:

amazon.com/author/therealbookgal ↗

> Copy link

Learn more about Author Page URLs

WHAT THESE AUTHOR CENTRAL CHANGES MEAN TO YOU

As you saw, when you first land on an Author Central page, it pushes the author bio out front and center, which wasn't the case on the older pages. This means your bio and your author photo are more important than ever. If you haven't refined your author bio or added a great author photo, now is a good time to do so.

The other element is how the books are staged on Author Central, leading with your most popular book right up front. Other titles can be sorted by number of reviews, price, release dates, and several other elements.

For now, it's a good idea to check your "new" Author Central page, refine your author bio and image, and make sure they're strong and represent your brand well.

YOUR AMAZON FOLLOWERS

Within your Author Central page, click on the Reports + Marketing tab. You'll see lots of data, which we'll get into next. But this tab also shows you your followers—readers who follow you and want to know when your next book is released! Promote your Amazon Follow link whenever you can; you can even add it to your website.

FARMING DATA FROM AMAZON AUTHOR CENTRAL

One of the major benefits of accessing your Author Central page is the data. Authors can now access helpful statistics about their pages, including sales numbers from both BookScan and Amazon data.

BookScan is the gold standard by which all your print sales are judged. Anyone with a BookScan account can access your sales data, unlike Amazon sales numbers, which aren't made public.

You can also check your author rank, which may show up on some book pages too.

Unlike BookScan data, your Author Rank takes into consideration your eBook *and* print sales, across all of Amazon and also within your genre, so Amazon will let you scroll down and see the breakdown specific to your market.

ADDING REVIEWS TO YOUR BOOK PAGE VIA AUTHOR CENTRAL

Dressing up the Amazon book page is a high priority for authors. It used to be that authors were at the mercy of reviewers or publishers providing details. That's not the case anymore. Now you can go in and add reviews *you* choose to help dress up the page.

Here's how: Once your books are listed on your author page after you've connected them to your account, click on the book title, and it will open to a page that lets you fill in all the back-end details such as your author interview and reviews. It's that easy. You can do the same with endorsements.

The editing possibilities in Amazon are sophisticated, so bold and italicize portions of your reviews, like headlines and names, whenever possible.

Amazon's editing tools work like Word's, making it easy to draw a potential reader's attention to a particular sentence or section of a review.

MONITORING REVIEWS ON AMAZON AUTHOR CENTRAL

You can monitor your reviews on Amazon from your Author Central page and see which are the most recent and which of your books were reviewed. This makes it easy to keep track of all of your recent reviews.

ANOTHER BOOST FOR YOUR BOOKS

Within the Author Central dashboard is an underused, little-known section that can enhance your books. This area includes sections for "From the Author," "From the Inside Flap," and more. I think it is often overlooked because authors don't realize they can get creative. The space can be used for more than just reviews. You can use it to add a range of fun, informative enhancements to your Author Central page. For example, you can develop your dream Q&A as a way to share all the information you wish the media or readers would ask, or as a smart way to work in a range of information that you couldn't fit into your book description.

A personal note from the author is a clever way to show readers why you're passionate about your subject or genre.

Another option is to include information about a contest you're running or to mention your social media addresses, website, and more.

I've seen some authors use this space to update their readers about other promotions they're doing, too. For example, when you run discounted promotions or a freebie, mention them here. Amazon says it takes up to 72 hours to update, but I've never had it take that long. Still, plan ahead because if the Amazon machine gets busy and the update you're making happens in a limited time frame, you'll want to set it up well ahead of the promo date.

AMAZON VIDEO SHORTS

I love this feature, and it's not just for readers to add video reviews of your book. It's also a great tool for authors to add enhanced content to their page.

For example, currently we're working with an attorney who was involved in a highly publicized case about GM concealing a known deadly issue with its cars because it was cheaper to be sued by consumers rather than recall the cars and correct the defect.

Sounds horrifying, doesn't it? In this instance, the attorney is putting up short clips of his experiences while working on and winning this case. His videos show what it was like to go up against a gorilla like GM and have clients who were parents who had lost children in accidents caused by the defects. In one video he talks briefly about the toll this case took on him and his family. I encouraged him to do these videos to provide readers with an emotional connection as well as a glimpse of what they might expect from the book.

Video shorts can be used for just about anything, from a quick "thank you for visiting my Amazon book page" to a detailed sense of where the story came from, why you wrote it, and so on.

Note: I added this to the Author Central chapter because Amazon removed the ability to add video from your Author Central page; instead you can access Amazon Video Shorts right from your book page! All of these videos (once they're approved by Amazon) will appear on your individual retail pages.

THE MOST OVERLOOKED AMAZON SALES TOOL: INTERNATIONAL AUTHOR CENTRAL PAGES!

Have you ever looked at your KDP sales dashboard and wondered how you can sell more books in other countries? We have a client who noticed she was selling a large number of books in Japan and wondered if she could rack up more sales there.

In addition to pitching specific blogs in those areas or doing advertising geared to that market, all of which requires time and money, you could also take a few minutes and claim your Author Central pages in those countries. It's quick and easy, and the best part is, all the international Author Central pages are the same.

First, here are the countries that do *not* have Author Central pages set up.

- Brazil
- Canada
- China
- Mexico
- Netherlands

These countries all list your book but don't have a page connecting all your titles. The irony is most of our authors don't sell a lot of books in these areas unless the book relates to that country specifically. For example, a book about Mexican heritage might do well on Amazon's website in Mexico.

Next, let's look at the countries that *do* have Author Central pages:

- France
- Japan
- United Kingdom
- Germany

A note regarding Japan's Author Central pages: You have to

register there. Just use the same username and password you use for the US site; it takes just a few clicks. Don't let the "new registration" deter you.

From there, the system will ask to verify your email; in fact, all the sites do this. Once your email is verified, you're good to go.

YOUR AUTHOR CENTRAL TOOLS

When setting up an International Author Central page, use the Chrome browser. It has a Translate button that is far more accurate than any others. It takes one quick step to translate a Japanese website into English. And English to Japanese.

To start, you'll need your bio. You can use whatever bio you created for yourself on your US page, but it can be worthwhile to adjust it to the country you're targeting. For example, let's say you have an international mystery that takes the reader from the UK to Germany and beyond. You might want to address that in your bio because the international connection could help pull in readers from the countries you mention.

GRABBING ALL YOUR BOOKS

The other fun piece is that the system is very good at grabbing all your books. Just click on the Books and start adding your books by either author name, ASIN or book title!

THE FINAL RESULT!

Here you can check out Author Central Pages across several countries. They're robust and engaging, and they keep all the author's books in one place so readers can easily find them.

- France: https://www.amazon.fr/-/e/B00AB0CHJQ
- Germany: https://www.amazon.de/-/e/B00AB0CHJQ
- Japan: https://www.amazon.co.jp/-/e/B00AB0CHJQ

- UK: https://www.amazon.co.uk/-/e/B00AB0CHJQ

HOW TO ACCESS THESE PAGES

To make it simple for you, here are the links to access and update each of your pages. Yes, it's that easy!

- France: https://authorcentral.amazon.fr/
- Germany: https://authorcentral.amazon.de/gp/home
- Japan: https://authorcentral.amazon.co.jp/gp/home
- UK: https://authorcentral.amazon.co.uk/gp/home

BUT DOES USING INTERNATIONAL AUTHOR CENTRAL SELL BOOKS?

Yes, it does. In fact, authors we've done this for have seen a substantial uptick in international market sales. If you're already selling books in these markets, this will help you gain even more sales. If you aren't selling books in, say, Germany, you might not see any immediate effect there. But it's still a fabulous thing to have, so update and optimize!

CREATIVE WAYS TO BOOST YOUR KEYWORD STRINGS

've spent quite a bit of time in this book discussing keyword strings, both how to find them and how to use them. I have talked about using keyword strings in your book description and subtitle, even using keyword strings in your title.

But what if not all these pieces are an option? Will your book tank?

Fortunately, the answer is no. Your book won't tank. However, having more keyword strings on your book page will help a good deal with sales.

What can you do? How about an author interview?

This simple tool—a quick, interesting interview with you, the fabulous author, available on your Author Page via Author Central —is a great way to enhance your keyword usage and include words you might not have been able to add otherwise.

My suggestion for the interview is to keep it interesting enough that readers will want to read the book. Adding content just to add more keyword strings won't necessarily hold readers' attention.

Ask a few questions—up to five—and answer them in such a way that you can use some of your keyword strings. You can also add keyword strings to the questions themselves.

DISCOUNTED EBOOK PROMOTIONS

Promoting your discounted eBook is an effective way to boost your exposure on Amazon and help spark the algorithm. Be aware, however, that not all price promotions are equally effective. It's more important to be strategic than to be fast. I used to talk about free eBook promotions, but I'm now finding that discounted eBooks do equally well—so long as the discount is substantial.

TIMING YOUR EBOOK PROMOTION

Ideally you should wait until your book has been up on the Amazon site for a while before you offer a price discount. I've found that waiting 90 days is best. If you're doing a price discount only, you can do that anytime, but if you're offering freebies, give your book's sales a chance to grow on its own.

PRICING AND REVIEW STRATEGIES

In addition to timing, pricing and reviews are two aspects of eBook promotion that can make or break sales.

Generally, I don't recommend starting any type of campaign like this (whether paid or free) without having *at least* eight to ten reviews on your page. With the many discount specials already offered, most consumers won't go for a free or heavily discounted eBook with a naked Amazon page (a page with no reviews).

Right after the eBook campaign, you'll continue to see a lot of traffic on your page, the residual momentum you created with the promotion. I've seen it last up to three days. If your book did well during the promotion period, this momentum will help it rise higher in your category, since the promotion helped trigger the internal Amazon algorithm.

If your promotion was a freebie, keep in mind that your book will switch to a different list; it goes over to the "free eBooks" side of Amazon. That means that it could hit bestseller status on that list, although since it's free, the term "bestseller" is more a nod to ranking, not book sales per se.

For free eBook promotions, the right post-freebie pricing when it returns to the paid category will help perpetuate this algorithm. If the book did well, it might be tempting to list it at a higher price. However, I recommend that you keep your pricing low during the days immediately following your free promotion. How low? It depends on how your book was priced in the first place, but generally I suggest you discount it by half for just three days.

This may seem counterintuitive. I mean, you want to make money, right? What better way to sell tons of books at full price than by capturing the tsunami of traffic finding its way to your page because of your freebie?

Obviously, you want sales, but you should be thinking long-term, not short-term. If you can boost your book within a category with the right pricing, it will help to trigger sales momentum you would never get otherwise. If you keep your book on your readers' radar screen by having it show up higher in the category, you'll have more long-term sales.

EBOOK PROMOTION

Even if everyone loves a good sale, you can't just put the book up on Amazon, mark it free, and call it a day. You have to promote it.

Many sites let you list your book for free (see below). During your promotion, you should also be on sites like X (formerly Twitter), sending messages, using hashtags, and pinging other accounts.

Here are websites and X accounts that would love to hear about your freebie, followed by a list of hashtag suggestions. Plan your freebie at least two weeks in advance, because sometimes listings require that much notice. Many of these sites will also let you promote your book if it's 99 cents, which is another great way to get your book out there. There are some paid listings, too. I've had success with BookBub.com, Kindle National Daily, and Book Gorilla.

FREE SITES WHERE YOU CAN LIST YOUR BOOK

https://katetilton.com/ultimate-list-sites-promote-free-ebook/
www.ereadernewstoday.com
www.pixelofink.com
www.indiesunlimited.com/freebie-friday
www.kindlenationdaily.com
www.totallyfreestuff.com
www.icravefreebies.com/contact
http://www.ebooklister.net/submit.php
www.kindlebookpromos.luckycinda.com/?page_id=283
www.thedigitalinkspot.blogspot.com.es/p/contact-us.html
www.freekindlefiction.blogspot.co.uk/p/tell-us-about-free-books.html
www.freebookshub.com/authors/
www.frugal-freebies.com
www.ereaderiq.com/about/
www.snickslist.com/books/place-ad/

www.awesomegang.com/submit-your-book
www.goodkindles.net/p/why-should-i-submit-my-book-here.html
https://bookgoodies.com/authors-start-here/
www.indiebookoftheday.com

X ACCOUNTS TO NOTIFY

@DigitalBkToday
@kindleebooks
@Kindlestuff
@KindlebookKing
@KindleFreeBook
@Freebookdude
@free
@free_kindle
@FreeReadFeed
@4FreeKindleBook
@FreeKindleStuff
@KindleUpdates
@Kindlestuff
@Kindlemysbook
@Kindle_Freebies
@100freebooks
@kindletop100
@kindleowners
@IndAuthorSucess
@FreeEbooksDaily
@AwesometasticBk
@Bookyrnextread
@Kindle_promo
@KindleDaily
@Bookbub

HASHTAGS TO USE

#free
#freekindle
#freebook
#kindlepromo
#freeebook

Discounted eBook promotions are a powerful way to boost your overall exposure on Amazon, plus they can earn more reviews to help populate the page. I love doing freebies and discounts. I've often seen big sales bursts after a campaign has ended. One of the main reasons for this burst is the residual traffic still going to your book page after the promo has ended.

You can also promote your book with special pricing. Kindle Countdown Deals offers an opportunity to promote special pricing across a few days. You pick the pricing, and you pick the days. Be aware, though, that the idea behind Kindle Countdown Deals is to literally count down via your pricing. If you start the deal at 99 cents, it goes up to $1.99 the next day, and so on until it's back at its regular price. We've found that too many different price points confuse the consumer. Pick one price, do Kindle Countdown Deals, and let it run for three to five days.

SUPPORTING YOUR PROMOTION WITH ADS

I always encourage authors to consider many ways to support their work. Don't make one book promotion strategy fend for itself. If you're planning a promotion, in addition to promoting it on sites that will list your book, or getting other accounts to post about it, consider supporting it with ads.

While Amazon ads and social media ads have their place, the platforms are pretty complex. If you already know how to run those kinds of ads, use them. But for those who are new to ads or not yet comfortable with them, I have a solution: BookBub ads.

BookBub ads, unlike BookBub promotions, are available to all authors without restrictions. BookBub is a site for eBook promotion, but it's more than that; it's a place for you to connect with readers (grab your author profile at www.bookbub.com). And it's a place to network with other authors!

HOW TO COMBAT THE DISAPPEARANCE OF AMAZON REVIEWS

Disappearing reviews on Amazon are a consistent problem for most authors. In fact, some of my older blog posts on our website that address this issue are among our most popular posts overall. This tells me that despite Amazon being less aggressive with its review pulls, many authors still wrestle with this problem. If you've faced this issue, these tips may help you deal with it. Keep in mind that if this concern is impacting your book regularly, there may be a broader issue with the book, and I'll address that as well.

PRESERVE WHAT YOU'VE ALREADY GOT

Here's the scenario: you've got a dozen new reviews and suddenly half of them are missing. What do you do?

My suggestion is to keep a close eye on new reviews as they pop up. There's an easy way to do this (especially if you have multiple books). Just access the Customer Reviews section on the back end of your Author Central page on Amazon. That tab will show all your reviews, across all of your books. Screen-grab this page regularly, and note when reviews are missing.

How does this help you? When reviews get pulled, you still have the actual review, which you can then repost to the Reviews tab under each specific book under Author Central.

You'll still lose the review on Amazon, but you've at least preserved it to add to your book page. I do this regularly—once a week if I'm in between book releases, and more frequently if I'm staying on top of a new book release.

SOMETIMES AMAZON HAS A GLITCH

Though Amazon would never admit this outright, its website isn't perfect. Glitches happen all the time. It's understandable with a site that is enormous.

The same is true for book reviews. Just last week three people told me their reviews had gotten pulled and they wondered why. The books were in different categories. The only unifying factor was that the reviews had all been posted around the same time. I emailed each person and told them to try reposting the review. Two of them did, and the reviews have gone live.

Bottom line: if some of your reviews are pulled (and you have the screen capture to verify this), write to Amazon to see what's going on, or call the company via the Help button in Author Central.

I find that if you're reasonable, polite, and patient, Amazon Author Central will gladly help you. I've contacted Author Central for all sorts of issues and have gotten assistance.

It's hard but don't be emotional. It's discouraging when your book is losing reviews, so you may want to give it a day or two before you tee up an email asking for help. But if you can ask in a calm and professional way, engaging in a conversation with Amazon could be helpful.

In some cases, you may find it was a random glitch. I've known authors to inquire about missing reviews on Amazon, and then get them all back. It's worth trying if you feel that the reviews you lost were from credible sources including legitimate book buyers/readers.

KEEP PUSHING FOR REVIEWS

Maybe this sounds obvious, but authors (at some point) stop pushing their readers for reviews. You can't replace reviews you've lost, and even if you are among the lucky ones who have never lost a single review, you'd like to keep adding to the number of reviews on Amazon, right?

There are several quick ways to do this.

The first is the Dear Reader letter in the back of the book. This letter thanks the readers for reading and invites them to review your book on Amazon.

The second is to simply ask for reviews. It is something authors rarely do, but those who do ask reap the benefits.

If you don't have a mailing list, consider putting out the request on social media, but do so in a way that makes your readers feel like they're truly helping you. Remind them how helpful reviews are to the buying process, how their voice matters, and how their input (good or bad) could help to persuade a buyer. Never ask for five-star reviews; just ask for an honest assessment of your book.

The issue of disappearing reviews is a frustrating ongoing issue, and often it doesn't seem like a fair fight. I've seen products on Amazon with a crazy number of extremely similar reviews; in one case all the reviews had the exact same wording and were all left up on the product page. But sadly, it's all part of doing business on Amazon, which is why I suggest the simple but powerful strategies of policing your reviews, continually getting new ones, and taking your issues to Amazon when you feel there's been an error.

TURNING YOUR BOOK INTO A 24/7 SALES TOOL

et your book go to work for you. Use the book itself to encourage reviews.

One of our clients, a first-time, unknown author, was ready to market her book. We knew that, given her genre—contemporary romance—the potential for receiving reviews was low. We decided to encourage reviews by having her write a request letter to her readers to include at the end of her book. In her letter, she politely asked for feedback and a review. She now has nearly 70 reviews on Amazon. Simple but effective!

She was a first-time author with no online history, and she self-published. Even with all those things working against her, she got tons of reviews. Were they all five-star? No, but let's face it, a book page populated with tons of five-star reviews is often considered suspect anyway. All her reviews were authentic, written by real readers with whom the author engaged. What's more, those readers are now part of her "tribe." She stays in touch with them and lets them know whenever another one of her books comes out.

For her second book, we encouraged her to actually write a letter explaining how tough it can be to get reviews and encouraging her readers to review her book(s) on Amazon and Goodreads. She also thanked them for buying her book.

The result was amazing. Here's the letter, if you'd like to try it out for yourself. Revise the style of the letter depending on whether you've written fiction or nonfiction. Otherwise, feel free to copy this or adapt it—whatever you feel works for you—but use it. It works!

> *Thank you for reading!*
>
> Dear Reader,
>
> I hope you enjoyed *Shelf Life: The Publicist,* book 2. I have to tell you, I really love the characters Mac and Kate. Many readers wrote to me, asking, "What's next for Nick?" Well, be sure to stay tuned, because the saga of publishing drama isn't quite over. Nick will be back in book 3. Will he find his happy ending? I sure hope so.
>
> When I wrote *The Publicist,* book 1, I got many letters from fans thanking me for the book. Some had opinions about Mac and Kate, while others rooted for Nick. As an author, I love feedback. Candidly, you're the reason I will explore Nick's future. So tell me what you liked, what you loved, even what you hated. I'd love to hear from you. You can write to me at authorchristinageorge@gmail.com and visit me on the web at www.thepublicistnovel.com.
>
> Finally, I need to ask a favor. If you're so inclined, I'd love it if you would post a review of *Shelf Life*. Loved it, hated it—I'd just like to hear your feedback. Reviews can be tough to come by these days, and you, the reader, have the power to make or break a book. If you have the time, here's a link to my author page, along with all my books on Amazon: http://amzn.to/19p3dNx
>
> Thank you so much for reading *Shelf Life,* and for spending time with me.
>
> In gratitude,
>
> Christina George

Just a few things about this letter.

First, you can't just ask for good reviews.

Second, many people may read this as an eBook, so put a live link in the book, preferably a link to your Amazon Author Central page. When you're putting your book together, you won't have the actual link to the Amazon page it's listed on. Of course, you want your readers to see all your books, not just the one they're reading.

Add this letter to the last page of your book, not the front matter. Many authors like to write letters to their readers, but that's not the purpose here. You want to thank them for reading a book they just finished. If your request is at the front, they'll forget about it by the time they get to the end.

THE BENEFITS OF CROSS-PROMOTION

Another way to engage readers is to attract them from one book to the next. Generally, when you get to the end of a book on Kindle, it will send you over to the book's page and ask you to rate it. One thing the Kindle device doesn't do is send readers to the actual author page on Amazon, where they can find out about the author's other books. Kindle is in the business of selling books, so referring you to the also-bought section makes sense for them, but the same doesn't apply to you. Cross-promoting your books is an invaluable sales strategy.

OTHER WAYS YOU CAN CROSS-PROMOTE YOUR BOOKS

- List your other titles with excerpts at the back of your book. If you have too many, pick two or three, and vary which ones you mention in each of your books, meaning that in book X you reference titles A and B, and in book Y you mention titles C and D, and so on.
- Create a special offer that links to your website or, ideally, takes people to a special page on your website directing them to your special offer. As a thank-you, consider giving a free download of one of your books or novellas;

or if you've written nonfiction, a workbook, a quiz, or a checklist. In exchange for this freebie, you get their email address. This does two things. First, the freebie builds goodwill with your reader, and second, you're collecting their email for future promotions.

REVIEW INCENTIVES

f you have a gift or swag that ties into your product, you are allowed to send it to the reviewer. Reviewers *love* swag, as long as it's classy and not junk.

Incentives can be a great way to pull in reviewers, so send swag with your book. We offered a book-themed tote bag to the first 25 reviewers on one book and ended up getting almost all 25 reviews overnight because fans were so eager to get the tote bag.

Be creative. There is a variety of amusing and often useful items, such as a tote bag, that can promote a book's location or theme or represent a protagonist's personality. You can also find items commonly associated with your topic. For example, a novel set in Belgium was accompanied by a small box of Belgian chocolates while a motivational title was sent with practical pocket journals.

Just make sure you tell your reviewers you want an honest review, good or bad.

Keep it on the up-and-up. One author was so desperate to get reviews he offered an all-expenses-paid cruise for the best review, but he had no intention of actually providing the cruise. While this wasn't illegal, it was unethical. The author got tons of reviews, but he also had several people post reviews on his Amazon page calling out his scam. That wasn't a smart approach in the end.

One of the best incentives you can offer your reviewers is to express sincere gratitude. Always, always, always send a thank-you, either with the book or after.

Even if you don't like the review, thank the reviewer anyway. You'll cast your net even wider if you do.

Reviewers talk. Be grateful, no matter what. They'll genuinely appreciate that.

GIFTING EBOOKS

ifting eBooks is a fun way to use the Amazon.com system. You can gift eBooks to reviewers who request an ePub copy of the book, or you can gift them to various readers to help generate buzz and drive sales.

Be sure to drop the price of the book before gifting, though, so the gifting process will cost you less. I generally drop the price of my book to 99 cents before gifting. While it would be nice to gift your book during your freebie giveaway time, Amazon won't let you. The book has to be at a certain price point—whatever pricing you determine.

Gifting a book does not mean everyone will actually download it because they can use the price of the book to buy something else. I keep the pricing low so that it's too much work to start shopping and find something else more appealing than downloading your book.

When you gift the book, Amazon will send you to a form you can fill out with any message you want to include. Just complete the form and hit "Send."

You will be charged per book you send, but you will *not* be paid royalties until the recipient downloads it. That means if they don't

see the email notification—if it winds up in spam or whatever—
you'll still be charged but won't get your cut. You can circumvent
this problem by sending the book to people you actually know.
They'll be more inclined to download it. Be sure to send them an
email in advance to let them know it's coming, so if it doesn't show
up in their inbox, they can check spam.

Gifting eBooks can help spike sales statistics, especially if
everyone downloads the book on the same day.

As a final tip, if you want to spike your book in a particular
category, encourage your friends or followers to download immediately so it'll have a greater impact on your Amazon presence!

BONUS RESOURCES

Here are some free downloads to help you get focused and organized, and start selling more books!

Monthly Book Marketing Planner: Fill this out to ensure you have a book promotion strategy laid out in advance, saving you the stress of coming up with ideas on the fly, or missing crucial book marketing opportunities altogether.
https://www.amarketingexpert.com/monthly-book-marketing-planner

Quarterly Amazon Planner: Feel confident that you're keeping up with all your Amazon updates and optimization strategies throughout the year.
https://www.amarketingexpert.com/quarterly-amazon-planner

Blog Outreach Tracker: Use this to keep track of your ongoing blogger pitching, requests, and more!
https://www.amarketingexpert.com/blog-outreach-tracker

Reader Profile Brainstorm: Save time, money, and a lot of guess-work; and avoid missed opportunities by creating a fresh reader profile that will help you zero in on where you need to focus your efforts and on the best sales angles to use for your buyer markets. https://www.amarketingexpert.com/reader-profile-brainstorm

SPECIAL OFFER!

Amazon Book Page Assessment
for only $100!

Your Amazon book page is your best chance at making a good impression, and then making a sale!

Your Amazon book page needs to account for shopper and buyer psychology, specific market interests and trends, along with seasonal highlights and sales angles. It's not in your best interest to "set it and forget it."

We can offer you feedback and recommendations to make your Amazon page stand out and make customers take notice!

Discount: $50 off retail price with
Code: authorformula24

Click Here to find out more
and secure your assessment!
https://www.amarketingexpert.com/product/amazon-book-page-assessment/

ABOUT PENNY C. SANSEVIERI & AUTHOR MARKETING EXPERTS, INC

Penny C. Sansevieri, founder and CEO of Author Marketing Experts, Inc., is a best-selling author and internationally recognized book marketing and media relations expert. She is an adjunct professor teaching self-publishing for NYU. She was named one of the top influencers of 2019 by *New York Metropolitan* Magazine.

Her company is one of the leaders in the publishing industry, and she has developed some of the most innovative Amazon optimization programs, as well as social media/internet book marketing campaigns. She is the author of 23 books, including *The Amazon Formula, From Book to Bestseller, How to Sell Your Books by the Truckload on Amazon, Revise and Re-Release Your Book, 5-Minute Book Marketing*, and *Red Hot Internet Publicity*, which has been called the "leading guide to everything Internet."

AME has had dozens of books on top bestseller lists, including *The New York Times, USA Today*, and *Wall Street Journal*.

To learn more about Penny's books or her promotional services, visit her website at www.amarketingexpert.com.